LPC Skills Online

Liz Polding & Jill Cripps

Oxford Institute of Legal Practice

OXFORD

UNIVERSITY PRESS

OXFORD
UNIVERSITY PRESS

Great Clarendon Street, Oxford OX2 6DP

Oxford University Press is a department of the University of Oxford.
It furthers the University's objective of excellence in research, scholarship,
and education by publishing worldwide in

Oxford New York

Auckland Cape Town Dar es Salaam Hong Kong Karachi
Kuala Lumpur Madrid Melbourne Mexico City Nairobi
New Delhi Shanghai Taipei Toronto

With offices in

Argentina Austria Brazil Chile Czech Republic France Greece
Guatemala Hungary Italy Japan Poland Portugal Singapore
South Korea Switzerland Thailand Turkey Ukraine Vietnam

Oxford is a registered trade mark of Oxford University Press
in the UK and in certain other countries

Published in the United States
by Oxford University Press Inc., New York

© Oxford University Press, 2010

British Library Cataloguing in Publication Data

Data available

Library of Congress Cataloging in Publication Data

Data available

Typeset by Newgen Imaging Systems (P) Ltd., Chennai, India
Printed in Great Britain
on acid-free paper by
Ashford Colour Press, Gosport, Hampshire

ISBN 978–0–19–953936–9

1 3 5 7 9 10 8 6 4 2

Preface

We wrote this resource (we hesitate to call it a book as we hope that the book part will be very much secondary to the interactive part) because this is what we would have liked to have had when we were training as solicitors. There are many good books available on this subject, but we firmly believe that there is nothing like activity for helping you to learn, especially when what you are learning is something practical like a legal skill.

Learning by experience is wonderful, but you need to be able to put your skills into practice in your assessments on the LPC and from the earliest days of your training contract if you want to impress your firm. We designed this resource so that you could get plenty of practice at the skills you need and that your firm wants you to have, with plenty of feedback so you can see how you are progressing and how you can perform even more effectively. We hope you find it useful as we know we would have done!

We would both like to thank our families for their support during the writing of this resource and everyone who gave us helpful feedback.

Liz Polding
Jill Cripps

Acknowledgements

Oxford University Press and the authors of this product would like to thank the following people who gave advice and reviewed the online exercises as well as various chapters of this book:

Ralph Camp, Hertfordshire University
Kate Campbell-Pilling, Sheffield University
Samantha Cornock, University of the West of England
Rachel E. Cooper, Sheffield University
Nick Dearden, Manchester Metropolitan University
Louise Douglas, Manchester Metropolitan University
Fiona Fargher, Liverpool John Moore's University
Lucy Floyd, Oxford Institute of Legal Practice
Helen Fox, Staffordshire University
Viv Ivins, University of Central Lancashire
Keith Gompertz, Birmingham City University
David Hartley, Birmingham City University
Russell Hewitson, Northumbria University
Lyn Jones, Manchester Metropolitan University
Martin Jones, University of Central Lancashire
Phil Knott, Nottingham Law School
Phil Millington, University of the West of England
Sheree Peaple, De Montfort University
Amanda Rees, Swansea University
Adrian Savage, Nottingham Law School
Emma Whewell, University of the West of England
Deborah Wotton, BPP Law School

In addition, we would like to thank the following practitioners who are featured online, talking about their experiences of legal skills and those who helped make it possible for Oxford University Press to film these practitioners:

Jamil Ahmed, Shanklys Solicitors Ltd, Manchester
Martin Bourne, Darbys Solicitors LLP, Oxford
Malcolm Hacking, Hacking Ashton LLP, Newcastle-under-Lyme
Shree Hindocha, Henmans LLP, Oxford
Jon Viner
Patrick Whetter, Henmans LLP, Oxford

Contents

Guided tour of this product   viii
The online exercises   xi
How to register   xiv
Other important features   xvi

Chapter 1   Introduction   1
Chapter 2   Reflective Learning   11
Chapter 3   Legal Writing   19
Chapter 4   Drafting   51
Chapter 5   Interviewing and Advising   71
Chapter 6   Advocacy   97
Chapter 7   Practical Legal Research   125

Index   153

Guided tour of this product

LPC Skills Online is a unique and innovative learning resource. This book will give you information on the principles behind the skills in question, but the exercises you will find online provide you with a wealth of learning materials. These varied and engaging exercises complete with feedback are designed to help you to practice the skills required on the Legal Practice Course. The web site will give you feedback on your performance, help you track your progress, and enable you to reflect on your learning. Above all, the exercises will support your classroom or workshop sessions and provide an interactive environment in which to prepare for your LPC assessments.

An animated Guided Tour of this product can be viewed on the homepage. Simply click on the 'Guided Tour' link on the LPC Skills Online homepage at **www.oxfordinteract.com/lpcskills**.

What can I find online?

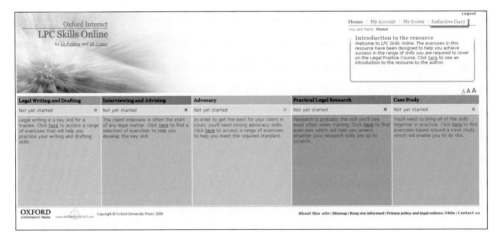

Interactive exercises

Over 60 interactive exercises covering all the skills required on the LPC can be found at: **www.oxfordinteract.com/lpcskills**

Once you've registered (for details on this, see p xiv), you'll be able to access all of these exercises. The web site is divided into five 'Skill Areas'. Four of these cover each of the following skills: Legal Writing and Drafting; Interviewing and Advising; Advocacy; and

Practical Legal Research. The fifth Skill Area, titled 'Case Study', contains exercises which use a case study to pull all of the skills together.

The five skill areas can be opened in any order, at any time during your course. Once you've started on a skill area, the web site will track your place, so that next time you log in you will be able to start again where you left off or choose to start somewhere new. This enables you to work through more than one Skill Area at a time, and makes sure that the web site is useful to you regardless of the structure of your LPC.

At the start of each Skill Area, you will see a film of the author, who will introduce the skill. In addition to this you can see a practitioner talking about how they use that skill in their day-to-day life as a practitioner. Use these sections to help you understand how you might use the skill in your training contract and see why it will be important for you to master.

Following these films, you will then be guided through a series of exercises which will help you develop and practice this skill. For more information on the types of exercise that you can expect to undertake, see page xi. If you score less than 50% in some exercises, you will be recommended to undertake a supplementary exercise which will give you more practice before you move on. You can 'skip' this supplementary exercise if you want to, but in order to get the best from this resource it is recommended that you undertake the exercise. If you score over 50%, you will still be given the opportunity to undertake the back-up exercise, but you will not be recommended to do so.

Your scores

The scores you achieve in each exercise will be recorded and can be viewed in the panel on the left of the screen on by clicking on the 'My Scores' link (see p xvii for more details). Use this facility to check on your progress and identify areas where you may need to ask for more support or help from your tutor.

Your account

Once you've registered your account, you can change your password at any time by clicking on the link to 'My Account' at the top of the page.

Reflective diary

Whenever you're online, you'll be able to reflect on your learning using the reflective diary that is built into the web site. Sometimes, the feedback in the exercises will prompt you to use this facility, but you can click on the link to the reflective diary at any point. The link will open a document for you to use to record your thoughts; this document can then be saved wherever you choose for future use. Reflecting on your learning can help you keep a record of your progress and this can be particularly useful in preparing for assessments or even for training contract interviews.

How should I use this book?

This book is divided into seven chapters. The first introduces you to the skills which are to be covered. The second concentrates on Reflective Learning. Use this chapter to help you make full use of the reflective diary facility that is available online. The chapters that follow mirror the five Skill Areas online. Section 7 on Practical Legal Research contains several problem questions which you will need to research before you complete the online exercises for this section. To get the most from the resources available online, it's advisable to read the relevant chapter in this book *before* attempting the relevant exercises.

The online exercises

LPC Skills Online features a range of interesting types of exercise, some involving video or audio material. All of the exercises have a practical focus and use realistic, but fictional scenarios, typical of situations that trainees would come across during their training contract. All exercises also provide feedback on the answers chosen, so you can understand why your answer was correct, incorrect, or partially correct.

Use the following pages to familiarise yourself with the types of exercises you will undertake online.

Matching

This exercise will require you to match a series of statements to a correct answer. For example, in Exercise 1 in the Writing and Drafting skill area, you'll be asked to identify which of a series of legal terms are archaic, and which are still in use.

True or false?

You'll be asked to identify various statements or words as correct (true) or incorrect (false). Exercise 2 in the Writing and Drafting skill area gives you a list of commonly misspelled words and asks you to identify which spellings are correct and incorrect.

Missing phrase

This type of exercise is used to give you practice at choosing the best way to phrase your writing. Some exercises like this will ask you to choose the most appropriate phrase for inclusion in a letter to a client; other, like Exercise 12 in the Writing and Drafting skill area will ask you to choose the most appropriately drafted clauses for inclusion in a Terms of Business document.

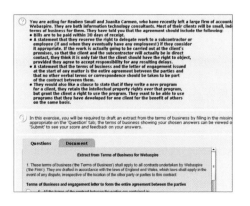

Multiple choice questions

It's likely that you will be familiar with this type of exercise. You'll be given a question, followed by a choice of answers. Some answers will be correct, others will be incorrect, and some answers will be partially correct to reflect the fact that, in practice, there is rarely one 'right answer'.

Constructing a document using multiple choice questions

This exercise is similar to the multiple choice questions with which you'll probably be familiar. Here, each possible answer takes the form of a paragraph from a document. When you select your answer, your paragraph will be added to the relevant document so that as you progress through the questions and answers, you're actually constructing a letter to a client, or a memo to a partner.

Audio or video material followed by multiple choice questions

These exercises will ask you to listen to an audio file or watch a short film and then answer questions about what you have seen. Sometimes you will be asked to make notes while you watch or listen. You may be asked to appraise the performance of an advocate in court, a trainee undertaking a client interview, or trainee's phone call to a client.

Constructing a document following audio or video material

This exercise combines the two types described above. You'll be asked to watch a short film or listed to an audio file. Sometimes, you'll be required to make notes as you watch or listen. Using multiple choice questions, you'll be asked to construct a document relevant to what you have seen or heard. For example, Exercise 7 in the Writing and Drafting skill area presents you with a recording of a suspect who has been arrested for drug dealing. You'll be asked to construct an attendance note based on what you have heard.

Making notes in a template during audio or video material

You'll listen to an audio file or short film, then be asked to make notes using template which features various headings. Use these exercises to make sure you can easily identify important information and also to practice taking notes in a professional context.

The web site will not provide you with a score for these exercises. You will need to appraise your own performance by comparing your notes with the example notes presented online.

Complete a flowchart

These exercises enable you to identify various stages of a process. For example, Exercise 1 in the Interviewing and Advising skill area will help you to identify the various steps you should take to ensure that a client interview

is effective. You'll be asked to move the various elements into the correct order.

Video selection

These exercises use a number of film clips. You'll be asked to select the 'next step' for the trainee or advocate involved in the film. Once you've chosen the path you think is most appropriate you'll be able to see the conse-

quences of your choice, and see why that choice is correct or incorrect.

Identifying key words

These exercises will require you to identify the 'keywords' you would use when researching a given legal problem.

How to register...

It's easy to register to use *LPC Skills Online*. Simply follow the steps below:

1. Tear off the perforated strip on the access token you'll find at the back of this book. Please be aware that by tearing off the strip, you are agreeing to the Terms and Conditions of Use and the Privacy Policy which can be found at www.oup.com/oxfordinteract/lpcskills/privacy. Once the perforated strip has been torn off, you will no longer be able to return the book to the place where you bought it. The access code you will find under perforated strip is unique, can only be used once, and is not transferable.

2. Log on to www.oxfordinteract.com/lpcskills

3. Follow the on-screen instructions to register your account. You'll be able to choose your own username and password which can be used for all subsequent log-ins. You will not need to use the access code again after this.

OXFORD UNIVERSITY PRESS *Subscriber Services*

Access Token Redemption

❖ **Token Activation - Step 1**

Information

This page enables you to activate a token for an Oxford University Press online product site using the unique activation code supplied. This is a 12 or 16 digit code that may have been issued to you with an Oxford University Press book, or via email. Please note: this code may be valid for a limited period only, so please check before using it.

Step 1:

Activating your token is a three step process, where you are initially required to enter your unique activation code before providing contact details.

* **Access Token:** [   ]

* **Type the letters:** [   ]

☐ * By checking this box and activating your token, you acknowledge that you have read and agreed to our **Licence Terms** and **Privacy Policy**

[Activate]

© Semantico 2009

4. That's it! You're now registered on *LPC Skills Online* and can log in at any time using the relevant link on the home page.

Oxford Interact

LPC Skills Online
by Liz Polding and Jill Cripps

A A A

Introducing LPC Skills Online

Login here

LPC Skills Online is a great support tool for learning the skills required on the Legal Practice Course. A short book which accompanies this site introduces students to the concepts behind the skills while a series of online interactive exercises, some featuring video and audio material, offer students a way to practise the skills required, preparing them for classroom sessions and assessments. Covering legal writing and drafting, advocacy, practical legal research, and interviewing, *LPC Skills Online* covers everything that the LPC student needs to know. Students are also given the chance to put the skills into practice in a realistic case study.

- *LPC Skills Online* offers 60 interactive exercises covering all of the skills required on the LPC in context of litigation, business law, and conveyancing, ensuring that students gain genuinely transferable knowledge of the skills necessary to successfully practice as a solicitor

- Video and audio material complements the exercises to provide a varied and interesting resource that is engaging. Videoed interviews with practitioners offer an insight into how the skills covered will be used during a training contract and in practice

- The innovative nature of the exercises and the associated feedback provides a truly interactive online learning environment which complements and builds on any existing course material written by lecturers

Take a guided tour...

Click here to take a guided tour and let us introduce you to the best that *LPC Skills Online* can offer.

Immediate scores and feedback

Did you know that *LPC Accounts Online* is also available? Like *LPC Skills Online*, this title consists of online, interactive exercises to help you develop your knowledge of accounts, as required on the Legal Practice Course. Click here for more details.

Existing users

Enter your username and password

Username [   ]
Password [   ]

[Login]

New users

So you've got your *LPC Skills Online* book, and want to redeem the access token it contains? Click here to register and create a username and password.

Forgotten your password?

Using this site

You can gain access to this website via a unique code which can be found at the back of the accompanying textbook. Buy the textbook here.

Registering your access code is very straightforward, but if you have any problems, please call Customer Services on +44 (0)1865 353705.

Other important features

'My Account'

Once you've registered with *LPC Skills Online*, and have started making your way through the exercises, you can change your password at any time or view your scores using the link to 'My Account'.

You can also use this area to change your password. Remember to keep your password secret as this holds the key to your personal access of this resource, and to information about your progress.

'My Scores'

As you complete the exercises, your scores are displayed on the left of the screen, but can also be accessed via the 'My scores' link at the top of the screen. If you repeat exercises within a skill area, the site will record the most recent score only. Use the 'My scores' link to export your scores into a spreadsheet or to email your scores to a lecturer.

www.**oxford**interact.com

■ **Introduction**

Reflective Learning

Legal Writing

Drafting

Interviewing and Advising

Advocacy

Practical Legal Research

Section 1

Introduction

Introduction

This book serves as an introduction to a set of interactive skills exercises. Many books now offer interactive exercises as a back-up, but in this book the emphasis is very firmly on the exercises, with the book playing a secondary role.

Most of what you need is contained in the exercises themselves, not the book which introduces the exercises. The philosophy behind this is that you learn better when you are doing something active, like completing an exercise, rather than something passive, like reading.

At the beginning of this book there is an introduction to the kind of exercises that you will encounter in this resource. We have tried to give you a variety of different types of exercise where possible, but inevitably many will take the form of a multiple choice exercise. This is to enable the system to give you some idea of how you are performing and to provide you with feedback. You can then see your scores, but neither the other students nor your tutor will have access to them. The resource is structured like this to give you plenty of feedback on how you are doing, together with suggested answers and ideas on how to improve so that you can make real progress.

1.1 Why do skills matter?

There is a temptation to dismiss skills as 'soft' and to emphasize legal knowledge at their expense. Your legal knowledge is important, but if you can't carry out tasks expected of you because you lack the skills (legal writing, research and so on) you will not impress your firm or your LPC provider and this will make it difficult for you to do well in your studies, your training contract and your career.

The UK Centre for Legal Education at Warwick University published a report on the skills of trainees who had completed the LPC. The author of the report, Amanda Fancourt, spoke to a number of law firms to determine their view on legal skills.

Full details of the study's findings are available at www.ukcle.ac.uk/research/ukcle/fancourt.html, but some of the key points are summarized below:

- Trainees' IT skills were generally regarded as good
- Research ability was satisfactory, but there seemed to be a tendency to take an academic rather than a practical approach
- There were concerns about the standards of written English, for example with regard to basic issues such as grammar, punctuation and spelling
- Some concerns were also expressed about a tendency to use too academic a style in presenting research. A tendency to informality when emailing was also raised as an issue by the firms contributing to the study
- With regard to drafting, trainees needed to ensure that they drafted documents that were consistent internally (for example, defined terms being used in the same way

throughout, no contradictions within the document and so on) and appropriate for clients' matters

Law firms will expect you to have mastered the skills you will learn on your LPC. If you are asked to draft a letter or a document, they will expect it to be of a reasonable standard. If you are asked to carry out research, they will expect you to be able to conduct it professionally and in a reasonable amount of time and so on.

In the short term, you will be assessed in the five legal skills as part of your LPC course. Clearly it is in your best interests to ensure that you pass those assessments and succeed on your course. If you do not take skills seriously and recognize that the skills you need to succeed on your LPC and in practice are different to those you needed to do well in your degree or conversion course, you are unlikely to perform well in this area.

The SRA's written standards

The Solicitors Regulation Authority (SRA) standards for skills can be found on their website www.sra.org.uk and give more detail about what is expected of each LPC graduate when they enter their training contract.

1.2 Skills assessment on the LPC

During your LPC, you can expect to be assessed on the following skills:

- Writing
- Drafting
- Interviewing and advising
- Practical legal research
- Advocacy

Each LPC provider will assess these skills in a slightly different way. Sometimes they will be integrated into the various compulsory subjects and sometimes they will be taught as discrete stand-alone subjects. For example, some providers assess drafting in the context of property law and practice, others in the context of litigation. Your provider should tell you how you will be assessed for each skill. Make sure that you check the information provided so that you are clear how you will be assessed for each skill. You should also familiarize yourself with any guidance, for example assessment criteria, issued by your provider to give yourself the best chance of doing well.

In most cases, you will have an opportunity to take a mock assessment before you undertake the actual assessment. It is very important to take advantage of this, not only because it will give you a good idea as to whether you are on the right track, but also because it will give you a chance to get some feedback on your work. The more closely you can replicate the assessment conditions under which you will take the real thing, the better. At the risk of stating the obvious, never collaborate on mock assessments as you will end up with a rather distorted view of how well you will cope in the actual assessment.

Because each provider assesses differently, the exercises in *LPC Skills Online* are spread across the compulsory subjects and the pervasive topics (these are subjects such as EU law, taxation, professional conduct and financial services). This is partly to give you the best chance to practise in the area in which you will be assessed. However, the breadth of coverage is also designed to help you grasp the transferable nature of each skill, by using them in a variety of contexts. This is intended to give you depth and breadth of experience, as well as a variety of different scenarios that will be interesting to use.

Summary Points

- Skills are important both for passing your LPC and for your training contract
- You will be assessed on your legal skills during your LPC
- The exercises provide you with feedback as you complete them
- The exercises are set in a variety of contexts to give you a broad-based experience
- Your LPC provider will give you guidance on the context in which they will assess you on your skills. Always read any guidance carefully to give yourself the best possible chance of success
- Take full advantage of any mock assessments offered by your provider, including any feedback afterwards

---

1.3 The structure of the resource

There are seven sections in this book. You should read this section (Section 1) and the reflective learning section (Section 2) before reading about the individual skills. Each skill has an introductory section which leads on to exercises associated with that skill.

Writing and drafting each have a section of their own. This is because writing and drafting are often assessed separately. However, these two skills overlap in many ways and were until recently treated as one integrated skill under the Law Society/SRA's written standards. They are therefore included in the same module of exercises.

The order in which you complete the modules of *LPC Skills Online* is irrelevant. Different LPC providers teach and assess each skill in a different order and each skill's module therefore stands alone. You are therefore likely to find some repetition of small points between sections. For example, the sections on Interviewing and Advocacy will both look at the issue of open and closed questions. This is to avoid the need for you to read the sections in a particular order or to refer from one section to another whilst reading.

The sections for each skill will give you more idea of how each module is structured, but in general, the system marks the exercises and gives you a score together with feedback on both individual choices and the final outcome. The exception to this general rule is a small number of exercises in which you are asked to take notes using a template from either an audio or a video recording. You are then asked to draft an attendance note. Due to the nature of the exercise, the system cannot mark your work and you will need either to assess it for yourself or ask a colleague to mark your paper while you do the same for them, using the suggested answer. This is useful practice and it is much more effective if you can work with a colleague.

The main benefit of *LPC Skills Online* therefore comes from carrying out the exercises. Reading is a passive learning method and it is acknowledged by educational theorists and researchers that active learning is far more effective. The exercises are designed to give you plenty of practice and an opportunity to learn not only from any errors you may make, but also from the mistakes made by the characters in each scenario. There are examples of each exercise and guidance on how to complete them in the first part of this book.

Each module begins with a brief introduction from one of the authors, followed by a short interview with a practitioner on the skills they expect from trainees.

You will then proceed to the exercises themselves. The system will remember where you were last time so that you need not start again every time you access the resource.

1.4 The exercises

In most of the exercises there will be questions with a definite right or wrong answer. Some questions will have more than one right answer or answers which are partially correct and deserve credit. The exercises will always tell you which applies and why, together with some feedback. This right/wrong/partially correct approach is often reflected in practice. It is also possible that more than one answer may be correct, as for example with drafting, where there may be a number of acceptable ways to draft a clause.

At the end of each exercise, you will be given your score, together with feedback and some advice on how to do better next time if appropriate. For some exercises there will be a supplementary exercise which you will be recommended to complete if you scored less than 50% in the initial exercise. You can choose to skip this supplementary exercise, but in order to get the most from *LPC Skills Online*, you should undertake it. Equally, if you score over 50%, you will still be given the opportunity to undertake this supplementary exercise if you would like to consolidate your knowledge.

In every exercise, you will be prompted to use your reflective diary (see Section 2 for more details) and consider what you have done. This is an important part of your learning experience and should always be completed to ensure that you have a thorough grasp of the points raised by each exercise before you move on.

In each section of this book, there is a 'map' of the exercises contained in that module. Most of the exercises build on the previous ones in that particular module. This means that the order in which you carry out the exercise is pre-set. In many exercises you can print off a suggested answer which you can retain in your portfolio if you decide to complete one or are required to do so.

The exercise maps show some exercises in shaded boxes. As explained above, you will be referred to one of these exercises as a back-up if you scored less than 50% in the original exercise. The arrows in the map show the path that you need to follow through the exercises.

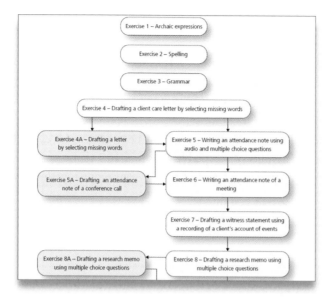

Note that where there are supplementary exercises, the arrows take you to the supplementary exercise (if your score was less than 50%) and then back to the 'main' exercises once the back-up has been completed. This is the case with all the modules although some modules have more supplementary exercises than others due to the nature of the subject matter. For example, Writing and Drafting has several such supplementary exercises, while Practical Legal Research only has a few.

The exercises in the Practical Legal Research module are slightly different to those elsewhere. In this module, you will carry out five exercises on key words, research method, using resources and presenting what you find before moving on to carry out some research to be 'marked' online. The questions for research are printed in the Practical Legal Research section so that you can use the hard copy while carrying out your research. Clearly having hard copy is useful for paper research, but it is also helpful for electronic research where you may find it difficult to shift backwards and forwards between two windows. For users with a slower connection on their computer, it may be impossible to display both the resource and the question at the same time. You should show your work as you would if you were handing it in to be assessed before going through the questions online to assess how you have performed and to receive feedback.

The exercises are designed to complement the face-to-face teaching that you receive from your LPC provider and not to replace it. Although practice in this way is very effective and can be very helpful, if you are in difficulties, there is no substitute for discussing the issue with a tutor. One of the preliminary steps that you can take if you do need to speak to your tutor is to use the exercises to narrow down your points of difficulty so that you can be focused in what you are asking.

1.5 The skills

Each of the skills has its own module, with the exception of Writing and Drafting, which are combined as explained earlier. Various different types of exercise are used in the modules and these are considered at the beginning of this book in the section on navigating your way through *LPC Skills Online*.

As discussed, the emphasis is very much on learning the skills by carrying out exercises, rather than by reading them. For example:

- In Writing and Drafting, you will practise the various different types of writing and drafting exercises that you might come across in practice including emails, letters, memos and documents
- In Interviewing, you will use a variety of exercises including audio and video exercises to give you experience of preparing for, conducting, recording and following up an interview
- In Advocacy, you will use more video-based exercises, some of which will allow you to choose what an advocate should do next in a variety of contexts
- In Practical Legal Research, you will look first at methods of research and then use the exercises in the Practical Legal Research section (see above) to practise and assess your research skills.

There is more detail on all these areas in the individual section for the skills.

1.6 The case study exercises

The final module should only be completed when you have finished all the other modules. The case study or consolidation module is intended to pull together all the skills which you have learnt so far in a single case study, much as you would in practice. In the case study module, you will follow a complete case from initial interview, through researching and writing a letter, drafting a standard form and finally being involved in a tribunal hearing.

The case study module should help you to see whether you are comfortable following a case through in this way or if there are areas of your performance which could be improved. It is designed so that you will use the information from one exercise to carry out the next and there are resources to print out at each stage to help you with this. It is deliberately not set in the context of a compulsory subject so that you can assess whether your skills really are strong enough for you to use them in an unfamiliar context as you might have to do in practice, for example when you start a training seat in an area of legal practice which you did not cover as one of your elective subjects on the LPC.

Summary Points

■ Read Sections 1 and 2 first followed by the section for the relevant skill before attempting the exercises for that skill

■ Writing and Drafting have separate sections, but one bank of exercises to ensure that the points made in the Writing exercises can be used in the Drafting exercises which build on them

■ The order in which the modules are completed is not set, so as to allow you to adapt it to your course. The consolidation module must, however, be attempted after all the other modules as it pulls them all together

■ The order of the exercises is fixed and includes supplementary exercises in some cases where your original score was less than 50% on an exercise

■ Some exercises may have more than one answer which will be marked as correct by the system. Some answers may be partially correct. The exercises will guide you

■ Where an exercise asks you to take notes, you will need to work with a partner or mark your own work

■ If in doubt, consult a tutor, but use your reflective diary and feedback to help you determine where you need help

1.7 Some conclusions

These skills exercises are intended to support the work you are carrying out as part of your face-to-face tuition. They should give you additional practice and a chance to really test your skills in your own time and at your own pace. Essentially, *LPC Skills Online* does what a textbook in the same area does, but with much more interaction, due to its very nature.

Remember that however helpful the exercises, you should not regard them as a substitute for what you are doing in your course, but as supporting that work. There are many other things that you can do to give yourself the best possible chance of doing well in your LPC assessments and impressing your firm.

For example:

■ If your provider records your performance in a skill (Advocacy and Interviewing and Advising are the most obvious candidates), make sure that you watch the results. You could watch them with a colleague and give each other feedback. If you can't bring yourself to do that, critique your own performance using what you have learnt from *LPC Skills Online* and your course

- If you are having problems, speak to a tutor at an early stage. Don't wait until you fail a skills assessment and have to resit it

- Accept that the skills are important and that you are unlikely to be able simply to perform them effectively without any practice or experience. You will need to learn how to do this, just as you have to learn how to apply your knowledge of the law and of legal practice to succeed in the substantive subjects on the LPC

- Take full advantage of any mock assessments and any feedback from your tutors or peers

- You should also accept that the LPC is a bridge between academic law and practice. Look critically at your approach and consider how you can adjust it to the new demands of the course and your training contract

- If you can practise your skills in another context – for example by mooting, entering interviewing competitions or by carrying out *pro bono* work, take the opportunity. It won't do your CV any harm either!

Finally, remember that everyone has to start somewhere. If your first few performances are not all that you had hoped they would be, learn what you can from them and use that in the next exercise. Feedback is always helpful in working out how you could do even better so please take it on board. If you feel you need more support, ask your tutor or, if the matter is technical, use the link and number of the technical support line on the site to get the help that you need.

Learning any new skill takes practice and legal skills are no exception. The more you practise, the more confident you will be that you can use these skills to good effect during your training contract and your career.

www.**oxford**interact.com

Introduction

■ **Reflective Learning**

Legal Writing

Drafting

Interviewing and Advising

Advocacy

Practical Legal Research

Section 2

Reflective Learning

Introduction

Learning is a very individual thing. Everyone has their own learning style and educational theory recognizes this phenomenon. All learning has, however, something in common. If the new facts, ideas or skills are to be really useful and form a sound foundation for further learning, *deep* learning must take place. Consider what happens when you research something and write about it, talk about it or discuss it with someone else whose views you take on board and then you work on that topic for a long period of time. The information, facts, ideas and skills will be learnt in a deep way so that they are retained and accessible for you to call upon and use as a basis for further learning.

Now think about what happens when you learn by rote, that is, you cram information without really understanding it or taking the time to think about it. This type of learning tends to happen just before an exam which you need to pass, but with which you never really engage. This type of learning is usually *shallow*. You have not really got to grips with the material and your learning is unlikely to be strong enough to use as a foundation for anything more.

The aim of *LPC Skills Online* is to help you acquire the first type of learning – deep learning – which you can use to succeed in both your LPC and your career as a lawyer. In the short term, of course, you need to pass your LPC assessments. You are more likely to do this if you can show that you have mastered the skills you practised in the exercises in enough depth to be able to take them forward into your career.

LPC Skills Online is intended to help you achieve this in a variety of ways. First of all, you will be carrying out exercises and therefore learning in an active, not a passive way. Extensive research on this issue has led to agreement among educational authorities that active learning is more interesting and effective than passive learning and, it is hoped, more enjoyable too!

The second way in which *LPC Skills Online* is designed to help you make your learning as deep and effective as possible is by means of the reflective diary. The reflective diary is designed to tap into another important factor in deep learning; reflection. Reflecting on your learning deepens your understanding and leads you to further development of the skill or knowledge.

2.1   Reflection

Reflection is a critical part of learning and is something that you probably do unconsciously anyway. It is about examining what you have learnt, considering how you will use it and whether it will change how you approach a similar problem in future; or even a different problem to which your new skill or knowledge can now be applied.

The reflective diary asks you to formalize this process by completing an entry for each exercise you complete. The diary can be completed using a template which gives you a structured framework for your reflection. This template asks you to consider what you have learnt using various open questions (questions like 'how?', 'why?', 'what?' and so on, which do not have 'yes' or 'no' answers). This may sound like an extra task – it isn't. The process of reflection is critical if you are really to master these skills (or any other learning for that matter).

If you don't reflect, you are only getting half the learning experience and half the benefit that you would otherwise obtain. Remember that this is something that you should be doing already, although it is possibly something that you do unconsciously. The reflective diary is just a learning tool to help you ensure that you really have understood what you have learnt and can apply it in other situations than the one you have just covered. Remember that in your assessments and in practice, you are going to be expected to deal with problems that don't come with a study guide pointing out how to tackle them. You will need to make those judgements and you cannot do that if you have only learnt your new skill to a level which allows you to deal with one particular situation. You need to go further; much further; and you can only do that if you take the time to really consider the exercises and how you can use what you have learnt from them.

You can include your exercises and reflections in an electronic or hard copy portfolio if you wish or if your provider requires. We will consider portfolios in a little more detail later.

The template for reflection is set out below and in your reflective diary; which is accessed using the link at the top right of your screen.

Don't feel compelled to write a particular amount. You may feel that a couple of lines is enough or you may have a lot more to say. However much you write, you will get much more out of the exercise if you consider it carefully.

2.2 Feedback

For each exercise, there is feedback on each choice that you make during the exercise and on your overall score at the end. Use this feedback to prompt your reflections:

- How do you feel about the feedback that you received?
- If you agree with it, why do you agree?
- If you did not agree with the feedback, consider why not and to what extent you disagree with what was said
- What messages have you received from the feedback and the exercise itself?

The feedback is also designed to reinforce some points and introduce new ones in the context of an exercise. Learning takes place best in a context so that you can see the concept applied and understand it better. There will therefore be some points that are not made in the text of this book, but which will arise or come to your attention in the exercises. Remember that the purpose of the book is to support the exercises, not the other way round.

2.1.1 Different kinds of feedback

There are a number of different kinds of feedback. The most obvious is the type that you will receive when you carry out the exercise. In your face-to-face tuition, you will receive feedback from your tutor. However, self-assessment using the reflective diary and feedback from your colleagues on the LPC and in practice can be equally useful. Considering your work together with a colleague can be very beneficial (although you cannot do this with assessments or practice assessments for obvious reasons). Your colleague may have considered things that you did not and vice versa. It is also possible that you made errors which were different from theirs and you can help each other address those errors. Information that you discuss with others is retained very effectively and discussion can be very helpful in consolidating your learning so do consider working with someone else. Although the exercises themselves should be attempted as a solo effort, discussion of the exercises afterwards could be really helpful.

2.3 The reflective diary

The reflective diary is a very flexible way of helping you to make sense of what you have learnt and to consider how you will use your new knowledge. If you have had difficulty with any of the exercises, and there are issues that you want to discuss with a tutor, you can use the reflective log to work out exactly what it is that you want to discuss. Your tutor can offer you far more help if you say 'I don't understand why this particular point was addressed in this way' than if you hand them the exercise and say 'I don't get it'.

You can also use it as a basis for discussion if you are working with others, or just use it as an internal dialogue to help you look more closely at your learning and make it more effective.

Whether you share your reflections with anyone is up to you, or, if your institution has a policy on this issue, that policy. For example, they may require you to keep a record of your reflections as part of a portfolio. However, remember that this is not an extra task to do as well as the exercise. Reflecting on your learning is a way of making sure that the work you put into the exercises is as productive and beneficial as possible. It is not an extra exercise, but the efficient and effective completion of the first exercise.

2.4 **Portfolios**

The Joint Information Systems Committee, an educational research body, and the Higher Education Authority, amongst others, are conducting research into the use of e-portfolios in professional education. The concept has already been adopted by a number of other professions including medicine (human and veterinary), architecture and engineering. The SRA is considering the use of learning logs and portfolios in legal education. The concept of compiling a portfolio of your work is not new, but its application to professional education is relatively recent. Portfolios are often linked to the concept of lifelong learning, with learners recording their learning in something portable that they can use throughout their education and professional development.

Compiling a portfolio of your work allows you to demonstrate that you have mastered particular skills and have applied legal knowledge. It allows you to demonstrate all the things that you have achieved in your training to the SRA, to the firm at which you are training, to a potential employer and, most importantly, to yourself.

2.5 **The template for reflection**

These headings are reproduced in your online reflective diary, but the headings are set out below for you to consider now, together with brief notes in italics after each heading. These notes will not appear in the online version.

Example

- **What was the exercise about?** *(Not just the topic, but the points that the exercise raised. For example, in an electronic research exercise, there will be points about searching such as the use of connectors)*

- **How did I do?** *(Not just your score, but how you found the exercise. Was it hard or straightforward? Why?)*

- **Did I meet my own expectations in this exercise?** *(Did you think you had done better or worse than you actually did? Why?)*

- **What did I learn from the exercise and the feedback?** *(Did the exercise challenge any preconceptions that you may have had? Did it give you any new ideas? What were the new ideas? Did it make you consider your approach to a problem of this type? Did you agree or disagree with the feedback? Why?)*

- **Would I do anything differently if I did the exercise again? If so, why?** *(If you were to start again, what changes would you make to your approach? What preconceptions would you get rid of and why? How would you change your answers and why?)*

- **What can I take from this exercise and where might I use this knowledge or skill in the future?** *(Consider what you will do with what you have learnt. You might want to consider how you would do things differently in situations of this type, but with different facts. What factors would make you do things differently, such as changes to the facts, different timings and so on? Knowledge and skills are only useful if you know how to apply them in different situations that you might encounter in an assessment or practice. Consider what these situations might be and how you would use your knowledge or skill to deal with them)*

- **Anything else?** *(Any other thoughts that you have which you haven't covered in the other questions)*

The reflective diary produces a Word document which you can either print out and include in a paper portfolio if you complete one, or save in an electronic portfolio if you have compiled one.

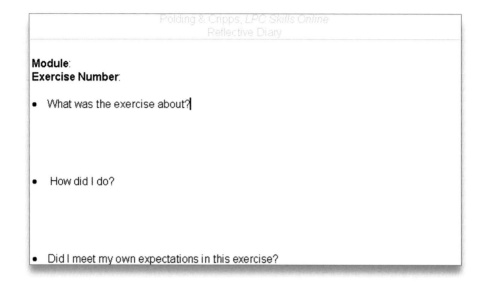

2.6 **Conclusions**

Reflection is an important part of any learning, but if you are to develop as a professional, you will need to develop a habit of reflection, that is , you will need to become a reflective practitioner. If you can do this, you will be able to deepen your knowledge and approach your client's matters with more assurance, building on what you learn and honing your skills.

In the shorter term, your LPC assessments will require you to demonstrate a sound knowledge of the skills you are to use in practice. If you can reflect honestly on your performances in all your skills and use your reflections to improve how you approach the skill and how you perform in it, you will stand a far better chance of being assessed as competent in the skill. If you can do this in the initial learning process and any practice assessments, rather than using the feedback from your assessment to help you improve in the resit, this has to be a better use of your time.

Make sure that you use the reflective diary every time. The exercises will prompt you to do this after every one and you should seize the opportunity and make your learning and your time really count.

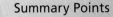

Summary Points

- Reflecting on your learning will help ensure deep learning; more effective and useful for you to take forward
- Reflecting is not an extra task; just the effective completion of the exercise
- Use your feedback to help you learn; don't just look at your mark
- Remember that there is more than one type of feedback. Honest feedback that you give yourself, feedback from a colleague and feedback from your tutor can all be useful
- Remember that what you learn has to be applied. Rote and shallow learning will not help when you have to apply your knowledge in a different context
- Even if you are not required to do so, consider compiling a portfolio of your work so that you can see how far you have come and, if necessary, demonstrate your achievements to a third party. Social networking sites such as elgg.org can support a web-based portfolio if your provider does not require you to make one as part of your course

www.**oxford**interact.com

Introduction

Reflective Learning

■ **Legal Writing**

Drafting

Interviewing and Advising

Advocacy

Practical Legal Research

Section 3

Legal Writing

Introduction

Legal writing is one of the five key skills on which you will be assessed during your LPC. When you begin your training contract, you will find that you use this skill many times each day. Your written work is also a permanent record of your performance in any matter in which you are involved.

A great deal of a lawyer's work involves writing in one form or another. Legal writing serves many different functions and part of the skill is to understand exactly what it is you are doing with any particular piece of writing.

This section will take you through some of the key points about legal writing. At the end of the Chapter, there is a section on the exercises for this skill. The interactive part of this skill is combined with the skill of drafting. Although they are separate skills, the skills needed to write effectively overlap with drafting skills and the interactive exercises are therefore combined, although the drafting elements are mainly towards the end of the interactive exercises.

Feedback from law firms obtained as part of a research project undertaken by the UK Centre for Legal Education is summarized in Amanda Fancourt's paper 'Hitting the Ground Running'. The overall view was that trainees' writing skills were often not up to scratch. For this reason, the interactive exercises include diagnostic tests to determine whether basic elements such as spelling, grammar and punctuation are up to the standards required by the profession. These issues are covered in exercises 1, 2 and 3. If you have any difficulties in this area, particularly if you have dyslexia, see your tutor.

The SRA's written standards

The standards for writing and drafting and all other areas of the LPC are available from the SRA website (www.sra.org.uk).

A note on assessment: This resource considers writing skills in the context of all the compulsory subjects. However, your provider may assess this skill in any one or more of these subjects. There is more general guidance in the Introductory section, but as a general rule, you will find it useful to review your examination guidance and the criteria used to assess the skill at an early stage. You can then consider your writing with these criteria in mind and use your reflective log to consider whether your work meets these criteria or whether you need to improve any areas of your performance.

3.1 The Writing and Drafting module

The 'map' below shows the writing and drafting online module. When you go online, you can check the 'What's new?' section to see if any new exercises have been added. As explained in the general introduction, the route through the exercises means that if you achieve less than 50% in an exercise, you will be prompted to carry out a 'supplementary exercise' before moving on.

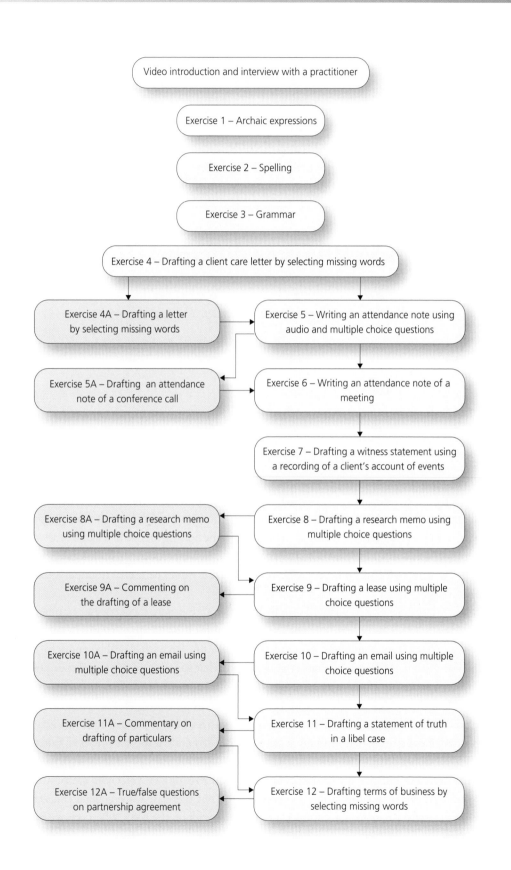

The exercises are mainly marked by the system, but some of the exercises in this module will require you to mark your own work by comparing it with the suggested answer. These exercises generally require you to make notes in a template, either when watching a video or when listening to an audio file.

Some of the exercises involve drafting a document, usually by selecting from a number of clauses and receiving feedback on your choices.

The exercises in shaded boxes are supplementary exercises which you will be prompted to complete before moving on in the event that you score less than 50% in the original exercise.

3.2 How is legal writing different?

There is no single type of legal writing. Every time you write anything during the course of your career, it will need to be tailored to suit the reader. You could be writing:

- A letter to explain a complex legal issue to your client

- A memo presenting your research findings to a partner

- An email to another professional

- A letter to an individual or a company on behalf of your client

- An attendance or meeting note

Each of these types of writing requires that you change your style slightly so that it is appropriate for the person who is to read it. The list above is not exhaustive, but one thing that we would definitely not include in our list is essay writing. This is the type of writing that you are likely to have used most often in your education, right through from primary school to higher education. Having spent so much time honing this skill, it can be very difficult for trainees to accept that this style of writing is not appropriate in their legal careers. In legal writing there are some key differences which it would be useful to understand at an early stage.

When writing an essay, you will usually be required to produce a particular number of words, say, 3,000. This is definitely not a requirement for legal writing. If you can say what you need to say in one sentence, or one paragraph or one page, that will be enough. The important thing with legal writing is to say exactly what you need to say to get your point across and no more. If you are, for example, presenting your research to a partner in a memo, lengthy paragraphs about why you think the law is wrong on this point are not required and will be ignored. Worse still, they may irritate the partner who is unlikely to appreciate having to plough through pages of beautifully crafted prose in order to find the point!

The exercises will give you examples of the kind of writing that you could expect to see in your legal career. Writing is not an exact science, but there are some general rules that will prove useful when you are completing a piece of work on the LPC, when you write an assessment and when you begin your training contract.

> ### Summary Points
>
> - There is more than one kind of legal writing
> - Legal writing in practice is not about essays
> - There is no minimum word limit – say what is needed and no more

3.3 Plain English

The use of plain English is key to good writing. It is very tempting to think that the extensive use of legal language is essential and that you will give authority to your writing by using a formal and complex style. The most important thing about any piece of writing is that it should make sense to the person who is to read it. If they cannot understand your writing, they cannot understand your point and you will have wasted their time. You will also have wasted your own time, as you will need to explain the issue to them again.

Plain English is essentially about saying what you mean in the most straightforward way possible. If a short phrase gets your point across, use one. Don't feel that you have to use lengthy phrases in order to sound like a 'real lawyer'. Many of the letters, memos etc that you write during your career will contain material which is legally complex. If the language in which you explain that material is unnecessarily complex, the result will be unintelligible! All the interactive exercises include an emphasis on plain English, but particularly exercise 4, in which you need to draft a letter to a dieat.

(?) Your principal, Louisa Burdett, has spoken to a client, James Polydore, on the phone. They have arranged a meeting to discuss Mr Polydore's matter, a boundary dispute, on **Wednesday the 28th of this month at 3:30 p.m.** The letter below contains some instructions as to how to get to your offices and confirms matters discussed so far. It also requests that the client bring various items with him to the meeting. There is no parking space available, but there is a nearby local authority car park. The letter is from your principal, but is signed by you in her absence.

(i) In this exercise, you will be required to fill in the missing words or phrases in the letter below. Choose the words or phrases you think are most appropriate on the 'Question' tab; the letter showing your chosen answers can be viewed on the 'Document' tab. When you're happy with your selections, click 'Submit' to see your score and feedback on your answers.

| Questions | Document |

Johnson Burdett Solicitors
25 Redmile Street
Lowtown
Somerset
SN48 2JH

Your Ref:

Our Ref: LB/jmo/82458

x/xx/20xx

Mr J Polydore
25 Whiles Lane
Lowtown
Somerset
SN49 3QM

Dear Mr Polydore

Re: Your legal matter

Further to...

◯   our recent telephone call

Essential Principles

Plain English does not mean informal English that is not grammatically correct. What it means is English that is correct, unambiguous and easy to understand.

3.3.1 Jargon

Jargon is essentially the use of words that mean something to those who are in a particular profession or trade, but not to lay people. For example, if a trainee solicitor told his supervisor that he was concerned that a trustee had breached his fiduciary duty, the supervisor would understand what was meant. If the trainee then wrote to the client stating that he considered that a particular action taken by the trustee 'breaches your fiduciary duty', but did not then go on to explain, the client is probably not going to understand what is meant.

The use of Latin and 'law French' used to be widespread in legal writing and no letter, even to a client, would be complete without using at least one such term. These terms are not used as much as they were and in many cases are regarded as archaic or old-fashioned. They are certainly not easy to understand for those who do not have legal training and in some cases for those who do. In many cases, there is a perfectly usable English alternative and that should be used where possible. In other cases, the meaning of a particular term is very precise and cannot readily be translated.

Exercise 1 asks you to identify archaic terms. You will find a legal dictionary very helpful here, particularly when identifying terms that are still in use because they have a very precise meaning. The feedback on this exercise should give you an idea of when these terms are avoidable and when you will still need to use them.

Some expressions commonly seen in older legal correspondence and drafting are now regarded as archaic. In order to make letters and documents clearer and less old-fashioned, these expressions are usually avoided in modern practice. However, there are some expressions which have a precise legal meaning and are therefore still in use because the alternative is lengthy and complex. In the exercise below, indicate whether the expressions listed are archaic and should be avoided or are still in use because of their precise legal meanings. The writing and drafting exercises contain more examples of this type of expression.

Drag the words 'Archaic' and 'Still in use' and drop them next to the statements to which you think they apply. When you're happy with your selection, click 'submit' to see feedback on your answers.

		Archaic	Still in use
Hereinbefore		Archaic	Still in use
Per stirpes		Archaic	Still in use
The said Mrs Hassan		Archaic	Still in use
It is hereby agreed		Archaic	Still in use
Jointly and severally		Archaic	Still in use

| Save | Print | | If you are happy with your selection | Submit | Clear all |

As a general rule, if a term is one that you would not have understood before you studied law, you should consider carefully whether to use it. For example, writing to your client about the *mens rea* for an offence which they have committed is unlikely to mean much to them. It is unlikely to have meant anything to you before you began your studies and you should therefore consider whether it is appropriate. Many archaic terms were removed from common use by the Woolf reforms, but even post-Woolf, there are still many terms that remain in use. For example an affidavit is now called a sworn statement in some areas of law, but remains an affidavit in others.

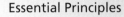

Essential Principles

Generally, there are three ways to approach jargon and archaic terms:

- If there is a plain English alternative, use that alternative
- If the term has a precise legal meaning which cannot be put into plain English easily, consider using the term, but explaining its meaning. For example if you are using a term in a document, explain its meaning in a covering letter
- If you are confident that the term will be understood by the reader, use it

Whatever approach you decide to take, the most important thing is that you are aware of the issue and take a considered approach. As you gain experience during your career you will do this automatically but in your LPC and training contract you will need to take a measured approach to help develop your writing skills.

3.3.2 Clarity

Clarity is essential to writing of any type – with the possible exception of some of the more abstract types of poetry! Clarity is particularly important in legal writing because ambiguity or saying something you did not intend to say can lead to a number of unpleasant consequences. If you write a letter to the solicitor on the other side in a contentious matter, ambiguity could lead to the court ruling against your client. If your client loses a case because of negligence on your part, they not likely to want you to act for them again and may well sue you.

As we have already considered, clarity through minimizing jargon and using plain English is important, but there are other ways of ensuring that your work is clear and easy for your reader to understand.

The length of your sentences can be important in determining whether your writing is clear or difficult to understand. As a general rule, longer sentences tend to be harder to read. The main reason for this is that they tend to contain many subclauses which can be difficult for the reader to follow. If a sentence is lengthy and deals with a number of different subjects, it is usually clearer to break it up into shorter sentences.

Example

Mr George Mifsud, who is married to my sister-in-law, Marina (she broke her leg last year while on holiday in Cyprus), told me that I could obtain a copy of the commentary on the epic poem – which Homer wrote in his last years – translated into Maltese, if I wished.

This is clearer if it is broken down into shorter sentences:

Example

Mr George Mifsud told me that I could obtain a copy of the commentary on Homer's later epic poem in Maltese if I wished. Mr Mifsud is married to my sister in law Marina. Marina broke her leg on holiday in Cyprus last year.

Although shorter sentences tend to be easier to read, you should not assume that it is always best to use short sentences every time. Using only short, punchy sentences can be just as difficult to read. For example, compare the two approaches below:

Example

She fell off the cliff. Her foot must have slipped. The grass was muddy. He could not have saved her. She died immediately.
He could not have saved her as she fell off the cliff and died immediately. Her foot must have slipped on the muddy grass.

Essential Principles

Generally, while shorter sentences tend to be clearer, varying the length of your sentences works better when you are writing more than a few lines. Where a sentence is very lengthy and runs to several lines, it is always worth considering whether it would be clearer if it were broken up into shorter sentences. Again, a great deal of making your writing work well is about reviewing it and asking yourself if your reader would find it easy to understand.

3.3.3 Grammar, spelling and punctuation

Most of what you write in practice will be typed on a computer, probably using a well-known software package which includes a spellchecker and a facility for checking grammar. This will obviously pick up many errors. However, it is important to ensure that you do not simply leave everything to the spellchecker. Remember that some words are spelt differently depending on the context and the spellchecker will not pick these up.

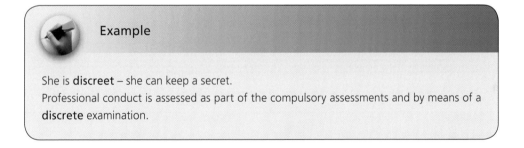

Example

She is **discreet** – she can keep a secret.
Professional conduct is assessed as part of the compulsory assessments and by means of a **discrete** examination.

Grammar, spelling and punctuation are important. If they are correct, they are not noticed. However, if they are incorrect, they convey an impression of sloppiness and inattention to detail. You may be an excellent lawyer with a keen eye for detail on legal matters, but if your writing contains errors, the client may feel that this tells them a great deal about your overall approach. This may cause them to lose confidence in you and to focus on your punctuation error, rather than on what you are actually saying in your letter.

Essential Principles

The features of plain English are:

- It is accurate (spelling, grammar and punctuation)
- It is clear and easy for the reader to understand
- Sentences are of an appropriate length
- Jargon is avoided wherever possible

At the end of the section, there is a list of further reading, including books on punctuation and grammar as well as a legal dictionary. It is not the purpose of *LPC Skills Online* to teach you the rules of grammar, spelling and punctuation. However, the interactive exercises on writing and drafting contain some diagnostic tests (exercises 1, 2 and 3) which will give you an indication of whether this area is a problem for you (see the screenshots below). If it is, you need to ensure that you address those problems so that they do not cause difficulties in your assessments on your LPC or prevent you from doing justice to your abilities in your training contract.

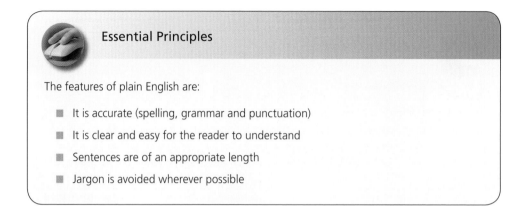

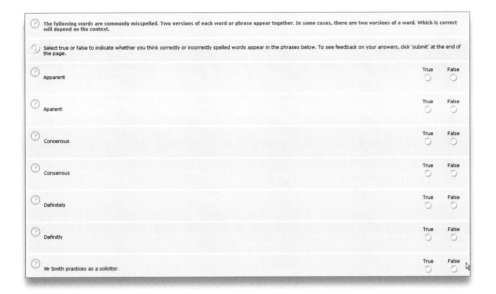

3.3.4 Detailed brevity

Detailed brevity sounds like a contradiction and, to some extent, it is. However, this sums up the point of good legal writing fairly neatly. What is required is that you get across your point in as many words as it requires and no more. However, it is also important to leave nothing out that is relevant or supports your statements.

Essential Principles

- Put in what you need to get your meaning across
- Don't leave out anything which is relevant to achieving that aim
- Leave out anything which is not relevant

When you are putting across an argument or setting out a record of research (see below), your reader should be able to follow easily. If there are particular facts that are important, do not be afraid to make use of bullet points to make them stand out. Be careful with bullet points and numbered lists, however. If you use them too much, they will not stand out. In addition, a letter or memo which relies too heavily on bullet points can look rather unprofessional. You will get an idea of how your firm likes things to be presented (see 'House style' below), but as a general rule use bullet points to make key points stand out. Bullet points can be particularly useful if you have a short list of points to emphasize.

3.4 Aiming for your audience

Whenever you write, you should always consider your reader. This will affect your decision on matters such as whether to cite cases or statutory authority in your text and the tone of your writing (see below).

As we considered above, you will have a number of different possible readers for your writing. The approach you take and the way that you express yourself will be different for a different audience.

Example

Compare the two paragraphs below:

'If your money is not refunded within 14 days of the letter to the solicitors for the mail order company, we shall be entitled to take them to court. As the goods that you bought are clearly faulty and you have sent them back within the time given in the contract, we seem to have a good case against them.'

'The goods in question are faulty and have been returned by our client within the contractual period. If our client does not receive a full refund in accordance with the terms of the contract we shall issue proceedings against your client.'

Although both paragraphs say approximately the same thing, they say it in very different ways. The interactive exercises cover this point in more detail but the underlying message is that you need to consider whether the intended reader will understand what you have written and also whether what you have written is appropriate for that reader. This is something that you will do automatically once you have had some experience. However, if you are aware of the issue and tailor your writing to your reader, the quality of the letters, memos and file notes that you give to your supervisor will give a better impression of your abilities than might otherwise be the case. Exercise 10 in the writing and drafting exercises will give you some practice at this.

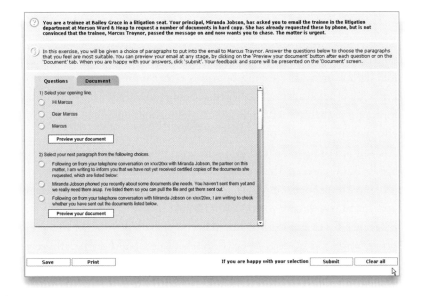

3.4.1 Tone

The tone of your writing is critical if you are to create a professional impression. In particular, the tone you use when writing to your client is important. If your letters are too 'chatty' and over-friendly, you will come across as unprofessional and casual. If your letters go too far the other way, you will appear rude and condescending.

> **Example**
>
> Compare the different versions of the same request below:
>
> 1) 'If you could send me the will within the next few days, that would be great as I can then get on with the application for the grant for the estate!'
>
> 2) 'Please send me the will without delay in order that I may progress the application for a grant in respect of the estate of the deceased.'
>
> 3) 'I would be grateful if you could send the will to me as soon as possible. This will enable me to make the application for a grant in relation to your late husband's estate.'

The client would probably find the first option rather casual and may feel that they are not being treated with respect. The second option is rather pompous and the client may feel that they are being ordered around, rather than being provided with a professional service. The third option is probably about right as it is polite, but makes it clear why it is important to receive the will as soon as possible.

When writing anything to be read by a colleague, it is also important to ensure that the tone of what you say is correct. The senior partner may not appreciate being told that he or she 'must' do something, for example. Your firm's approach to writing to colleagues should become apparent to you during your training contract. If the style is usually quite casual between colleagues, for example, this should become obvious from the files on which you work. If you are unsure, it is better to be reasonably formal (although definitely not pompous) than to err on the side of being too casual.

When you are writing to another solicitor, the tone of your letters will vary depending on the subject of your letter or email. If the matter is contentious, you would usually expect the tone to be much more formal (see 'Forms of address' below for more detail). Where the matter is non-contentious, the tone is often rather less formal (although you would not expect it to be casual). Generally, you should be guided by your firm's house style on this point. Exercise 8 in the writing and drafting exercises will give you some practice at writing a memo to a partner.

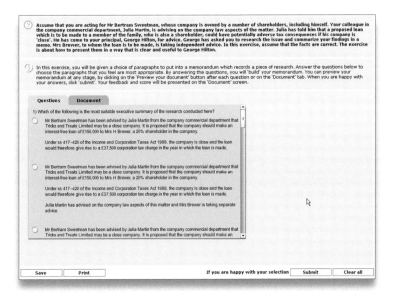

3.4.2 Citing authority

Citing authority is something that you will be used to doing from your legal studies so far. If you are to make a statement or give advice, there must be some authority for this and, if you were writing a paper, you would give a case or statutory reference to prove your point.

When you are writing in practice, you will still want authority for your points, but you will not always cite it explicitly. The decision as to whether to do this or not depends on who is to read your writing. If you were writing a record of research for a partner in your firm, you would always expect to cite authority specifically. Similarly, if you were writing to a solicitor or other professional, you would expect to cite authority.

If, however, you were writing to a client, you would generally not expect to do anything more than tell the client what the law says insofar as it is relevant to their matter.

Example

Compare the two paragraphs below:

'Mrs Graham will be entitled to make a claim under the Inheritance (Provision for Family and Dependents) Act 1975, provided that she is within the categories of potential applicant set out in s 1. An extract from s 1 is set out below.' (More appropriate for a colleague.)

'The law in this area means that Mrs Graham might be able to make a claim against the estate if she fits the necessary criteria. The categories of possible claimants are set out below.' (More appropriate for a client.)

Some clients are obviously more sophisticated than others and some will want to know the law, either because they have some legal knowledge or because they are particularly interested. As a general rule, clients do not want lots of detail about the legislation or cases. They want to know how the law affects them and how you, as their solicitor, propose to address the problem and solve it.

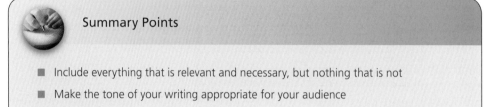

Summary Points

- Include everything that is relevant and necessary, but nothing that is not
- Make the tone of your writing appropriate for your audience
- Use citation appropriately

3.5 Practical points

You will very quickly learn what resources you have within your firm for producing a piece of writing. You may, for example, be required to dictate letters and memos for typing by a legal secretary. If this is the case, you will need to develop two aspects of your writing skills. You will need to learn to plan what you are going to say so that you can get something coherent onto your Dictaphone. You will need to ensure that you proofread everything that comes back from a secretary and either amend it yourself or mark it up for the secretary to amend. Be particularly careful about words that sound very similar (see exercise 2) as they can be easily missed when proofreading.

If you do not type your work yourself, you may want to bear in mind the following points:

- The clearer your dictation, the easier it is for the secretary to understand it and the more accurate it is likely to be as a result
- If you change your mind, cough or otherwise put something onto tape that you don't want, it is usually possible to rewind slightly and tape over it
- If you don't understand how the equipment you are given for dictating works, ask, don't struggle
- If you are putting something into a secretary's in-tray, mark it clearly and state whether it is urgent. If it is not urgent, give a date by which you need it. Most firms will have a system for doing this and you may need to fill out a form to accompany your tape

- When you are marking up a draft of a letter, if the amendment is very small, it may be easier to do it yourself if you can

- When marking amendments on a draft, write clearly. If you have a number of amendments to a passage, consider putting the extra text onto a separate sheet, marking clearly where it is to go in the main document

- If you delete something that you later wish to reinstate, underline it and write 'stet' alongside it. This means 'let it stand' and is widely used in this context

If you are typing your own letters, you will need to become quite critical of your own work as everything you write will need to be proofread to ensure that it is correct. If you are typing your own work, your firm will often have templates of letters, memos etc. If they don't, set up your own templates so that you don't have to think about issues such as fonts and formatting every time you write anything. Again, be careful about proofreading as it is particularly difficult to check your own work as there is always a danger that you will see what you expect to see – see exercise 2.

3.5.1 Digital dictation and voice recognition software

Digital dictation is much like dictation on a normal Dictaphone, except that the record is digital and is loaded onto your computer or your firm's network to be replayed and transcribed by a secretary once you have uploaded it. The files can also be attached to an email if your firm uses a remote typing service.

Some firms use voice recognition software packages that can type what you say straight into a document, rather than producing a tape which has to be transcribed by someone else such as a secretary. These have the added advantage of allowing you to amend the document at the time you draft it. These packages have advanced a great deal in the past few years and will no doubt continue to develop as they become more popular and come down in price.

If your firm uses either of these packages, you should receive training on how to use it effectively once you have started your training contract.

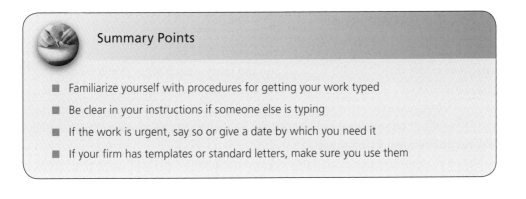

Summary Points

- Familiarize yourself with procedures for getting your work typed
- Be clear in your instructions if someone else is typing
- If the work is urgent, say so or give a date by which you need it
- If your firm has templates or standard letters, make sure you use them

3.6　Letters

Having considered general guidance that applies to all types of writing, we need to look at some specific types of writing that you will certainly come across during your career. You will undoubtedly write hundreds, if not thousands, of letters during your legal career. This form of communication has not yet been ousted by email, although many letters are now sent by email and many communications that were previously sent in a letter are now sent by email.

Letter writing is still a big part of a solicitor's work and knowing how to write a professional, well-constructed letter provides you with a chance to demonstrate your skill in your training contract. Exercise 4 in the writing and drafting exercises will give you the opportunity to practise writing a letter to a client.

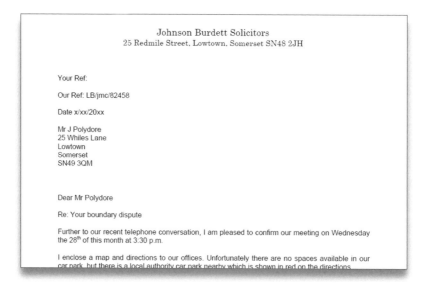

Johnson Burdett Solicitors
25 Redmile Street, Lowtown, Somerset SN48 2JH

Your Ref:

Our Ref: LB/jmc/82458

Date x/xx/20xx

Mr J Polydore
25 Whiles Lane
Lowtown
Somerset
SN49 3QM

Dear Mr Polydore

Re: Your boundary dispute

Further to our recent telephone conversation, I am pleased to confirm our meeting on Wednesday the 28th of this month at 3:30 p.m.

I enclose a map and directions to our offices. Unfortunately there are no spaces available in our car park, but there is a local authority car park nearby which is shown in red on the directions

3.6.1　References

The rules considered earlier regarding the tone and style of your writing clearly apply to letters. Your reader should be able to see clearly and fairly quickly what the letter is about. If it is a letter in response to a letter from a business or another firm and they have a reference on their letter, make sure that you use it in your reply. Your reference will usually include the file number and something to identify the fee-earner; usually their initials. Your firm will have its own standard format.

It is also customary to include a title below the salutation (eg Dear Sir) so that it is clear what the letter is about and which client it concerns. When writing to an individual client, you would still do this as it needs to be clear to them why you are writing and what about. For example, if you were acting for them by drafting their will and in the purchase of their house, state which matter the letter relates to in the title.

3.6.2 Headings

Although your firm will have a standard template for letters (see 'House style' below), in general it will be acceptable, and usually a good idea, to make use of headings in your letter if it is longer than a couple of paragraphs. Headings break up the text and make it easy for your reader to navigate around the letter. Where the matter is complex, letters of advice can run to several pages and headings can make a big difference to the ease with which your letter can be read.

As previously considered, you could use bullet points in a letter, but generally they should be used sparingly, to add emphasis or to set out lists.

3.6.3 The first paragraph

It is often the case that the first paragraph of a letter will contain what is sometimes called 'an executive summary'. This provides the reader with the main point of the letter, with the detail contained in the later paragraphs. Clearly this is only going to be required where the letter needs such a summary; a one-page letter which has very little detail does not require a separate summary; but it can be very useful. It helps you to focus on the main points and it also ensures that the client is then reading the rest of the letter in light of your summary. This can often make something complex much easier to follow.

3.6.4 The body of the letter

The letter needs to flow logically from paragraph to paragraph, ensuring that you do not jump about between topics or leave out links in your chain of reasoning. If your first draft looks a little disordered, rearrange the paragraphs so that it makes more sense. The letter should form a coherent whole, not a series of disjointed paragraphs.

Although many of the letters you write will be very short, they still need to be ordered logically, but clearly this takes more practice with longer letters as you are dealing with far more information which must be presented logically.

Exercise 3 in the case study gives you the opportunity to practise putting together the body of a letter to a client.

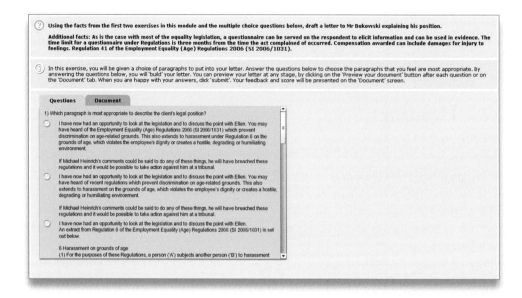

3.6.5 Final paragraphs

Often the final paragraph is the place where you would set out anything that needs to be done, either by you, or by the client. If you are using a summary at the beginning of the letter, this can be done in the summary if you prefer. It is important to be clear as to what is to happen and also to keep the tone appropriate, particularly if you are asking the client to do something.

3.6.6 Enclosures

Enclosures such as documents or forms should be listed, usually after the signature at the end of the letter. This serves as a checklist for both the sender and the receiver so that it is clear what was sent and what should be received.

3.6.7 Forms of address

There are a number of forms of address that can be used in letters. There are some general rules about which to use and when but some of the main points are set out in the following table.

Opening	Closing	When would you use it?
Dear Sir	Yours faithfully	When you are not addressing the recipient by name – for example the solicitors on the other side in your matter. You would also use this form of address when sending a letter in the name of the firm.
Dear Mr Smith	Yours sincerely	When you are writing from a named individual to a named individual.
Dear Mr Smith	Yours truly	See 'yours sincerely'. This format is less common than 'yours sincerely', but be guided by your firm's house style.

Where the letter is from the firm, be careful to use the pronoun 'we' throughout the letter (rather than 'I', as the letter is not from you but written on behalf of the firm). The letter should also be signed either in the name of the firm or in your name with a statement that it is signed 'on behalf of Smith & Jones'.

When you draft a letter to go out in someone else's name (your supervisor, for example), you can sign it 'per pro' (usually abbreviated to 'pp') the other person if they do not actually sign it themselves. Examples of all these points are included in the interactive exercises.

3.6.8 Client care

When you take instructions from a new client, or, in some cases, new instructions from an existing client, you will generally send out a 'client care' or 'engagement' letter which sets out certain information which the SRA requires us to give our clients. Your firm will have standard paragraphs containing this information, which you should incorporate into your letter in an appropriate place. In some cases, a separate client care letter will be sent. Your firm will have its own procedures on this issue, but be aware that you will need to consider it when writing to your client.

> **Summary Points**
>
> ■ Ensure that it is clear what the letter is about and be careful about how you address the client
>
> ■ Who is the letter from – you, a colleague or the firm?
>
> ■ Use a summary so that the key points are obvious
>
> ■ Use plain English
>
> ■ If you will be doing something or you need the client to do something, make this clear

3.7 Memos

Before the advent of email, memos were the main form of written communication between colleagues in a law firm. Although they are not used as much as they were, they are still useful, primarily as a method of presenting research – see below. Your firm will have a standard template for memos.

As with other forms of written communication, using headings to break up the text and make it easier to follow is helpful to your reader. You will also see the use of the executive summary in longer memos. This is used in the same way as an executive summary in a letter. The key points are summarized at the beginning or end of the memo, with the detail of those points set out in the rest of the memo, signposted by clear headings.

Memos are not signed, but your name and the names of those to whom the memo is addressed will usually appear at the top of the first page, along with the date and the subject of the memo.

3.8 Presenting your research

Memos are generally used as a way of presenting your research. As a trainee, you will frequently be asked to carry out research and present it to one or more colleagues. You will quite often be asked to do this under pressure of time, because the advice the solicitor is to give the client depends on the outcome of your research.

3.8.1 Structure

When you present your research, it should be clear where you found your results and your conclusions should follow logically from them. This is one occasion where you would always cite authority for anything you say. Your firm may have a standard format for research memos, but broadly your memo will contain the following:

- Executive summary
- The facts – often summarized so that the key points are clear
- The law – remember that it may not be immediately obvious which areas of law are involved and it will help your reader if you identify them explicitly
- The client's objectives – what it is that the client wants to achieve
- The research path (often the detail of this will be on an accompanying record card if your firm uses them)
- Your conclusion
- Your advice based on that conclusion

As previously considered, a plain English approach should be used in memos as it would be in all other forms of written communication.

Exercise 8 gives an example of how you would present your findings to a colleague.

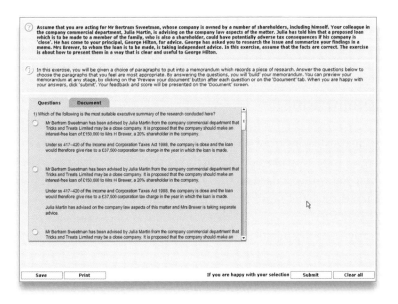

Remember that your audience has a high level of legal knowledge and a relatively small amount of time in which to read your memo. In particular, ensure that you make your text clear and easy to read, using headings and bullet points to allow your reader to pick out key points. You should also ensure that you give clear authority for any points you make including full references for any cases.

3.8.2 Research paths

Make sure that your research path can be followed easily and is complete, without steps missed out. This does not mean that you must put in pages and pages of detail, but you should enable your reader to follow your trail and pick up particular points if they wish. For example, if you refer to *Halsbury's Laws*, say which paragraph and how you found it. You should also show clearly in your memo that you have checked updating resources such as 'Is it in force?'. See the Practical Legal Research section and exercises for more details on updating and research paths.

3.8.3 Copying and pasting

If you are quoting from a case or statute, resist the temptation to simply copy and paste great chunks of material from an online resource. Be selective. If you have read through a section of a statute which has 28 subsections, three of which support your conclusion and contain wording which is important for your reader to see, it will be clearer to include only those three subsections or extracts from those three subsections in your memo. If you simply copy and paste the whole section, you may end up with several pages of text, only some of which is actually useful. You may find that you are asked either to edit the memo and take out the extraneous material or that you annoy the fee-earner and waste an opportunity to demonstrate your professional capabilities.

3.8.4 Conclusions

When drawing conclusions from your research, remember that you are not telling your senior colleagues what they must do. Be careful of the tone of what you write and always remember that you will be judged on the quality of what you produce. Trainees who tell the senior partner that s/he 'must' do something are not often popular!

In your conclusions and advice, if there are practical steps that need to be taken, set them out clearly – possibly in bullet point form.

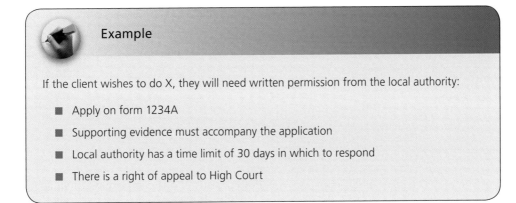

Example

If the client wishes to do X, they will need written permission from the local authority:

- Apply on form 1234A
- Supporting evidence must accompany the application
- Local authority has a time limit of 30 days in which to respond
- There is a right of appeal to High Court

Overall, your memo should be clear, easy to follow and accurate. The fairly obvious point to bear in mind is that the person asking you to carry out the research is asking you because they do not know the answer. In previous research that you carried out in your academic studies, your work would be marked by someone who knew the answer and could tell you if it was right or wrong. That is not the case with a research memo in a practice context so accuracy and clear presentation are important.

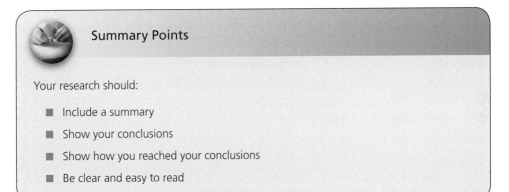

Summary Points

Your research should:

- Include a summary
- Show your conclusions
- Show how you reached your conclusions
- Be clear and easy to read

3.9 Attendance notes

As a trainee, you will frequently be asked to produce a note of meetings and court hearings. Throughout your career you will write attendance notes of your own meetings and telephone calls. The purpose of these notes is to provide an accurate record of what was said and any action points that arise. They may also be used to compile witness statements and affidavits in contentious matters. Exercise 7 will give you the opportunity to practise compiling an attendance note in a criminal matter; you will also be able to see the resulting witness statement.

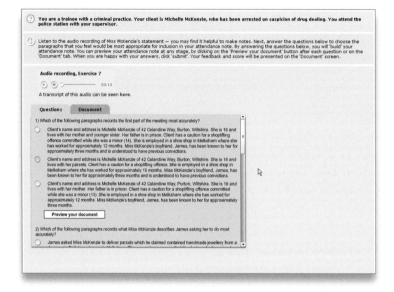

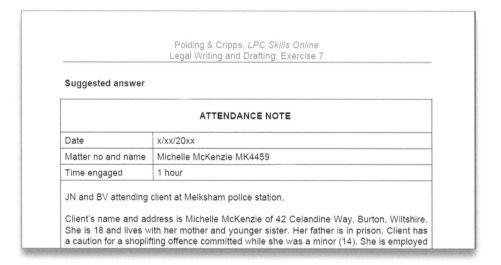

When making notes, remember that a verbatim (ie word-for-word) note is not usually required. Generally, what is required is a record which includes all the relevant detail, but does not include anything that is not necessary. For example, if the client repeats themselves and makes the same point three times, you would only record the point once. Irrelevance and unnecessary detail should be left out. If you are unsure, it is best to include something, rather than leaving it out, but remember that if you write vast amounts it is possible that points will be overlooked because there is simply too much material.

3.9.1 Meetings

Taking notes in lectures is similar to taking meeting notes. If you try to record every word, you will almost certainly not manage to do this and will miss important points. You should aim to take down as much as you can without losing the thread of what is being discussed. Pay particular attention to times, dates, names and other key factual information.

If you are sitting in on a meeting, you will not generally be involved in the discussion and can therefore take fuller notes. If you are conducting an interview with a client, you will need to try and take some notes during your discussion, but without disengaging from the client and making them feel that you are not really listening. In these circumstances your notes will be brief, often just a few key points. However, once the client has given their account of their problem, you should check the key points with them and ask them supplementary questions in order to ensure that you have everything you need in order to advise. It is possible to ask these questions as the interview progresses, but be careful that in doing so you do not make the client feel as though they are being interrogated or prevented from telling their story in their own words.

In addition to providing a record of the meeting or interview, your meeting note should include the following information:

- The date
- The time the meeting began and ended and the time engaged (this is particularly important for billing and in contentious matters when recovering your costs)
- Who was present (and the time they arrived if they were not present throughout)
- Details of who gave any information, eg Mrs Smith said that the car went through the red light, Mr Smith noticed that the car had no rear number plate

The main purpose of any attendance note is to ensure that anyone; for example your successor trainee if you move seats and pass on a matter; could pick up your file and have a clear idea of what is happening and what needs to be done. If possible, try to complete your meeting note within, at most, a few days of the meeting. If you delay, not only will your file be incomplete, but you may find that your notes do not make quite as much sense as they did when you first made them!

3.9.2 Telephone attendance notes

Telephone attendance notes are very similar to meeting notes, although while you are actually on the phone, it is rather more difficult to make all but the briefest notes. The details of the call, including the start and end times and the time engaged, should be included, as should the details of the parties to the call.

Whether the attendance note is typed will depend on what is usual practice for your firm. Many firms provide attendance note pads and handwritten notes are acceptable; others require typed notes.

As with a meeting note, it is probably unrealistic to try and take down every word, not least because you will be speaking to the person at the same time. Try to get the main points down and do not be afraid to ask the client to repeat something if you did not quite hear it.

It is generally helpful to include a summary of what was agreed at the end of your note, including a list of any points that need to be actioned, not least as a reminder to you of what needs to be done.

Exercise 5 will give you the opportunity to practise taking an attendance note in the case of a phone call.

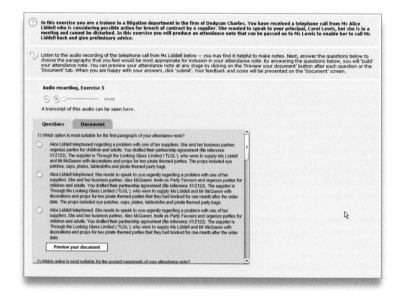

3.9.3 Sitting behind counsel

Trainees will often be asked to 'sit behind counsel' in open court hearings where they will not have a right of audience. The purpose of this exercise is to provide an accurate record of the hearing for the file and for your supervisor so that they know what points were raised, anything said by the judge and the details of the order so that it can be checked when it is received.

The points already considered about trying to take down every word also apply here, but accuracy is very important and you will not be able to ask the judge to repeat anything they say. You can check key points with counsel, but remember that you are paying for counsel's time and this should be confined to checking small points rather than going over the entire hearing again.

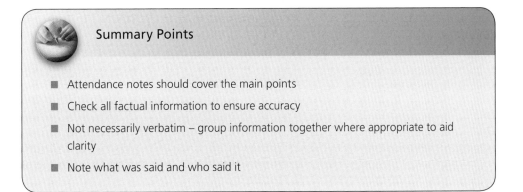

Summary Points

- Attendance notes should cover the main points
- Check all factual information to ensure accuracy
- Not necessarily verbatim – group information together where appropriate to aid clarity
- Note what was said and who said it

3.10 Emails

Increasingly, email is being used in practice where letters and memos might previously have been used. Email is often used socially and there can be a tendency to be too casual in terms of format and tone. There are a number of points to bear in mind when using email:

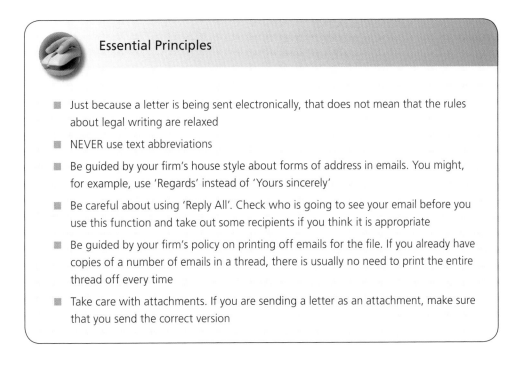

Essential Principles

- Just because a letter is being sent electronically, that does not mean that the rules about legal writing are relaxed
- NEVER use text abbreviations
- Be guided by your firm's house style about forms of address in emails. You might, for example, use 'Regards' instead of 'Yours sincerely'
- Be careful about using 'Reply All'. Check who is going to see your email before you use this function and take out some recipients if you think it is appropriate
- Be guided by your firm's policy on printing off emails for the file. If you already have copies of a number of emails in a thread, there is usually no need to print the entire thread off every time
- Take care with attachments. If you are sending a letter as an attachment, make sure that you send the correct version

Exercise 10 will give you the chance to practise drafting an email to a trainee at a different firm.

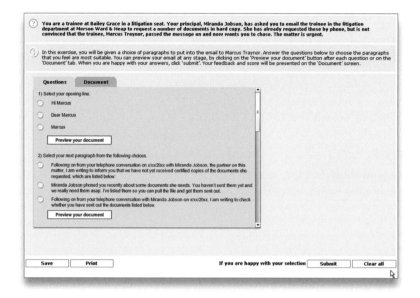

3.11   House style

Your firm will have a house style for most written communications. This will cover the font style and size, the style of headings and so on. In many cases, you will have a template for your letters, memos etc which you will use if you are typing them yourself and which a secretary will use if your typing is done for you.

House style may also cover points such as layout and the method of presentation of research. Your firm will, in most cases, have standard letters for matters such as probate. For example, when writing to banks to request a statement of the deceased's account at the date of death, the wording of the letter is the same each time apart from the details of the deceased and the bank concerned. If there are standard letters available, use them, rather than drafting new ones from scratch and wasting costs.

3.12   Proofreading

Before you finalize any written communication, always proofread. Small mistakes give a poor impression, even if they do not have serious legal consequences. In a letter to a client or a memo to a partner, the quality of your work makes a statement about your professionalism. If your work is full of small mistakes in grammar and spelling or contains typographical errors, you will give the impression of being inattentive to detail and careless. Careful proofreading can help ensure that your work is presented to best advantage and that there is nothing to detract from the points you are making.

3.13 The exercises

LPC Skills Online is designed to work with your course. Your tutor may guide you as to when you should do the exercises, but it is recommended that you read this section before attempting them. As with all the modules in this resource, when you access for the first time you will see a short video introduction, followed by an interview with a practitioner who will give you their view of how trainees perform in this area and what you could do to improve your skills.

A diagram showing a 'map' of the online exercises is included at the start of this section. The first three exercises are diagnostic and cover grammar, spelling and archaic language. If you have difficulty with these exercises, you should speak to your tutor.

The exercises build on each other and they will all cover a number of the points contained in this section. The best way to learn any new skill is to practise. After each exercise, use the feedback you have been given and your reflective diary (see the relevant section in this book) to deepen your learning and determine what points you can use in other exercises and in your career.

The exercises cover letters, memos, emails, attendance notes and drafting. The exercises should give you plenty of practice and give you a good idea of where you need to focus in order to improve your writing for your assessments and your legal career. If you have any questions, speak to your tutor.

The guide to the online exercises at p. 6 of this book, the 'Guided tour to the web site' at p. X, and the online 'Guided hour' give the details of what you should expect from each type of exercise and how to address any potential problems.

3.14 Conclusions

The purpose of any writing is to communicate. Using plain English, taking care with clarity and ensuring that the tone of your writing is appropriate will ensure that your writing gets your points across effectively and gives positive messages about your abilities and professionalism. Small errors can undermine what you say and divert attention away from what you are actually saying. Attention to detail and careful proofreading can help to make sure that this does not happen.

If you feel you need further support in this area, speak to your tutor. You can also learn more from the books set out below. *Fowler's Modern English Usage* is a sound reference work, while *Eats, Shoots and Leaves* achieves the impossible by making punctuation funny! For issues with spelling, consult any dictionary and remember that while the spellchecker can pick up some errors, it is not infallible and is never a substitute for proofreading.

Further reading

RW Burchfield (ed), *The New Fowler's Modern English Usage* (3rd edn rev OUP, Oxford 2005)

Lynne Truss, *Eats, Shoots and Leaves: The Zero Tolerance Approach to Punctuation* (Profile, London 2003)

Elizabeth A. Martin and Jonathan Law, *A Dictionary of Law* (OUP, Oxford 2006)

www.**oxford**interact.com

Introduction

Reflective Learning

Legal Writing

■ **Drafting**

Interviewing and Advising

Advocacy

Practical Legal Research

Section 4

Drafting

Introduction

Writing and drafting are very closely linked, but are in fact two skills, with separate assessments. During your career, you will draft a wide variety of documents in a number of different situations. Once you become more experienced, you will become familiar with the documents that feature most often in your area of law. The most obvious example is real property, where you will draft many leases, transfers and so on, but may still occasionally come across examples of transactions where the drafting is unusual. Often this will be because the circumstances are unusual and the drafting has to be amended to address the issues that this raises.

During your training contract, you will be involved in drafting different types of document in each area of your training. For example, if you are working with the litigation department, you might be called upon to draft any number of documents in relation to cases which actually go to court or those which settle through mediation or out of court. The Civil Procedure Rules, which govern the conduct of civil matters and will therefore be important to drafting in that area of practice, are covered in the litigation module of your LPC.

The important thing to remember in drafting is that there is no 'one size fits all' approach. Each document is different, just as each case is different. In most cases, these differences will not be sufficiently important to need significant amendment to the document that you are drafting. However, the skill that you need to develop includes the ability to judge when to amend and how.

Drafting has changed enormously in the last century. There are some obvious reasons for this, such as the arrival of computers, which make it easier to draft and amend documents. The other major difference is that the legal profession itself has changed.

A century ago, you might have drafted a bespoke document for each client, taking many hours to do so, but producing something perfect and individually crafted. However, law firms now charge, in general, on a time basis. Because of this change, the cost of producing a bespoke, individually drafted document every time would be beyond the means of most clients.

There is therefore a more procedural approach to drafting, using precedents so that the basic form of a typical document in that type of transaction is already completed. This reduces the time spent on drafting to some extent, but still requires the same levels of skill and understanding from the solicitor or trainee who is doing the drafting (see 'Precedents' below).

4.1 Plain English drafting

The principles of plain English that were considered in the section on writing apply equally to drafting, but with some special points. For example, most documents will not contain punctuation, other than brackets and quotation marks to show definitions – see below. If there is to be no or minimal punctuation in a document, you will need to be very careful to ensure that there is no ambiguity about your drafting; clarity becomes doubly important.

When you are writing a letter or a memo, clarity is important because you need to ensure that you get your point across. With drafting, there is an added dimension to the issue of clarity. If what you draft is ambiguous, or if you fail to include a point in your draft, there are likely to be unintended consequences. For example, if you draft a will which does not dispose of the entire estate, at least some of your client's property will pass under the intestacy rules.

When you are drafting, you therefore need to think not only about the clarity of what you are drafting, but whether you have provided for as many possibilities as you can. Drafting can often be time-consuming as you need to think carefully about what you are trying to achieve and about what you are trying to avoid. However long the process, it is unlikely to take as long as trying to sort out the results of poor drafting which has led to litigation or negligence claims.

Summary Points

- Plain English is equally important in drafting as in writing
- Punctuation is often not used in documents
- Clarity is key for an effective document; it must be unambiguous
- Drafting should cover all eventualities. Thinking time is vital

4.2 What is a document?

This may sound like a really silly question – surely it's obvious? A document in this context is a piece of writing which brings about a legal outcome. Legal documents contain various elements, but the content will generally follow the structure set out below:

Introduction or title – Some documents will have a front sheet which sets out the parties and a description of the document. The date will often be included here and elsewhere in the document. *Never fill in a date until you are certain that it is correct to do so. Often documents will be signed before they are dated. Adding the date makes the document 'live'. When sending documents out to be signed, but not dated, some solicitors will write 'Do not date' in pencil over the space where the date is to go at various points in the document to prevent the client from inadvertently bringing the document into effect prematurely.*

Definitions – This section says what terms you are going to use and how they are to be interpreted in your document – see below for more detail.

Body of the document, including the operative clause – This contains most of the detail of what your document is about and its various provisions. The operative clause is the most important thing here. The operative clause is what makes your document effective, or indeed makes it do anything at all! For example, in a legal mortgage, you need actually to state that your document is a charge by way of legal mortgage over a property. If you are selling shares in a company, your document needs to state explicitly that this is an agreement for the sale and purchase of shares in Company X. *This may sound as though you are being required to state the obvious – surely the document's function is apparent from its terms? Possibly, but in legal drafting, stating the obvious is essential. Leaving important things to be implied is dangerous and potentially negligent. Think about what your operative clause should be for every document you draft. Ask yourself what it is that you are seeking to achieve. If the document is a will, state that it is a will. If you are drafting a partnership agreement, say so.*

Schedules – For longer documents, there may be schedules dealing with, for example, the list of assets on a business sale, detailed provisions about particular areas such as tax, lists of properties included in a development, rights granted and reserved and landlord's and tenant's covenants in a lease, financial details and so on. The relevant clauses will then refer to the appropriate schedules.

4.2.1 Definitions

In most documents you will use definitions to ensure clarity and to avoid having to repeat large chunks of text each time you wish to use a term. Set out below are two ways of defining a property:

 Example

A The property known as Flat 21, 46 Arcadia Avenue London W1 4RF
B The property known as Flat 21, 46 Arcadia Avenue London W1 4RF ('the Property')

In option A, you will need to write out the address of the property in full each time you use it, which in a lease or transfer could be several times. It is far more straightforward, and normal practice, to use option B. This allows you to define the term once and then simply use the capitalized version thereafter. Using a capitalized term tells your reader that this term has been defined at some point and that it is therefore to be read in accordance with that definition.

There are two ways of defining a term, and the option you choose will depend on the type of document you are drafting. In a longer commercial document, you would expect to see a definitions section, which sets out all the definitions used in your document, usually in alphabetical order. If you insert a clause which uses a new term repeatedly, ensure that you add your definition of that term to the definitions section. In a shorter, less formal document, or in a letter, you might define terms as you use them. In this case, the term is set out as in option B above, with the definition set out in the text, followed by the term that is to be used as a type of shorthand for that definition in brackets and quotes and with a capital letter. For example, in exercise 9, you will be asked to define terms as part of your draft of a residential lease.

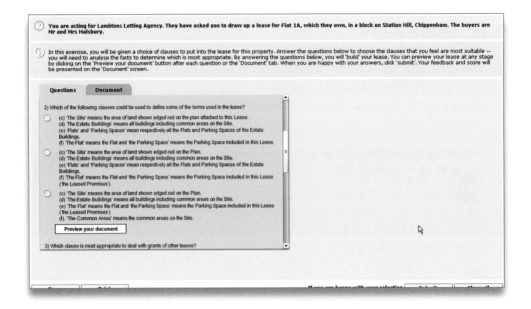

If you are amending a document, or drafting a new clause, ensure that you are using the defined term correctly. Checking the definitions section when you draft a new clause will help to ensure that you do not introduce a new, contradictory definition into your document in error.

Summary Points

■ Ensure that your document states what it is and includes an operative clause

■ Define any terms you intend to use in a particular way, for example 'the Tenant', 'the Company'

■ For longer documents, use a definitions section

4.3 Thinking through the consequences of what you draft

Many of the most common points that you need to address will be included in a precedent (see below). However, you always need to understand what the document says and its effect. In many cases, you will need to explain its effect and individual clauses to clients, either in writing or verbally.

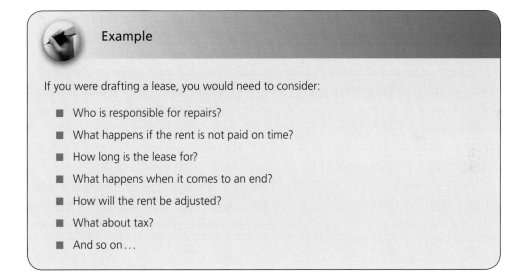

Essential Principles

When drafting any clause, you should consider:

- What it is that you are trying to achieve
- Whether your clause achieves that objective
- Whether it could have other consequences, either on its own, or when considered with other clauses
- Whether it is clear and unambiguous

Often the best way to do this is to think about what would happen in a variety of circumstances.

Example

If you were drafting a lease, you would need to consider:

- Who is responsible for repairs?
- What happens if the rent is not paid on time?
- How long is the lease for?
- What happens when it comes to an end?
- How will the rent be adjusted?
- What about tax?
- And so on...

Drafting which causes problems does so usually because it has not been thought through and the solicitor drafting the document has not considered what would happen in the situation which has arisen. Careful consideration when drafting will help to ensure that your document achieves your client's objectives and has no unintended consequences. Exercise 12 gives you the opportunity to practise this.

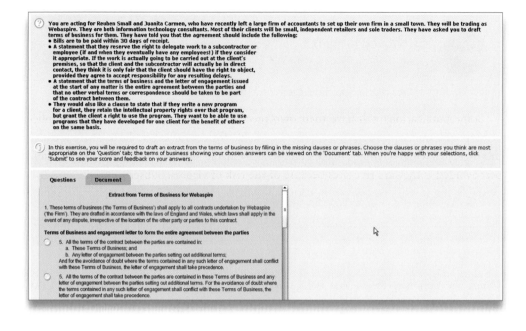

4.3.1 Using precedents

The move from bespoke drafting to quicker and less costly alternatives has involved the use of precedents. Precedents provide you with a structure and most of the key clauses which deal with many of the major points are already in place. For example, a precedent lease would deal with all of the points considered above and many others. However, precedents are not a substitute for clear, focused thinking by the solicitor. It is important to remember that a precedent is where you start the process of drafting, not where you finish.

There are many sources of precedents. Which precedents you have access to will depend on your firm. The *Encyclopaedia of Forms and Precedents* (EFP) is a common reference work to which the law library at your LPC provider will often have access, either electronically or in hard copy, or possibly both. Your local Law Society library will also normally have a copy of the EFP. Each volume of the EFP contains precedents grouped together by subject matter. The index will give you a helpful steer on whether there is a precedent that you can adapt to your matter, or a similar precedent that will give you some ideas to enable you to draft something yourself if your situation is very unusual. *Kelly's Draftsman* is used for forms and precedents in a similar way.

Your firm will often have a set or bank of precedents for the type of work that it carries out. Larger firms may have professional support lawyers who will review and update precedents. In other firms, you may be asked to carry out this task. If your firm has a precedent for what you want to draft, you should always use that precedent rather than going to the EFP, mainly because the precedent will be in house style. It is likely that your firm will require that you use the firm's precedents and turn to the EFP only when you have to do so.

There are many other volumes of precedents aimed at different areas of practice such as company commercial law, probate, and land law. You will become familiar with these resources in your training contract. They are not listed here as it would be impossible to cover every publication and, of course, those that are available to you will depend on your firm.

Some publications will have their own precedents. For example, PLC has a number of corporate and commercial precedents available for use by subscribers. There are also internet sites which claim to make precedents available to download. These are probably best avoided if they are free sites because of the risk of viruses. Subscription sites are also available, but it will be a matter for your firm whether you are able to make use of these.

4.3.2 Adapting a precedent

As discussed, using precedents can be dangerous if you are not careful. The first few drafting exercises that you carry out are likely to be time-consuming as the precedent will be unfamiliar to you and you will need to read it carefully before you can adapt it to suit your client's needs.

The point of using a precedent is that you do not need to reinvent the wheel each time you draft, but that you can and should amend a precedent as you consider appropriate. You should never be afraid to draft additions or amendments which make the document fit your client's purpose better. In some cases, you will have to draft a clause from scratch, in others, there will already be a clause in the precedent, but you need to insert text into it or remove text to adapt the precedent. For example, in exercise 11, you will use a precedent for particulars of claim and select clauses to include to adapt it for use in your client's case.

You are a trainee in a litigation seat in the firm of Maple Baker Charles, a Bristol firm whose address is 42 Clifton Down, Bristol BS3 7HJ. The partner in charge of your matter is Fiona Fingle. You have been instructed by your principal to draw up particulars of claim in a defamation action.

A recent book Plump Fiction, published by Grumbly Grossmere Limited, publishers, of 18 Back Lane, Rotherhithe, London SE16 4MJ, has made the bestseller list. In the book there is a character called Matilda Trumpeter, who is ridiculed for her weight problems, including some rather graphic accounts of bulimic episodes which are mocked in particular detail. Her morals are also called into question, with some graphic passages of the character's adultery with a number of Hollywood producers.

Your client is the actress Matilda Bugler of The Bird House, Swallows Lane, Box, Wiltshire SN13 2TP, who advises you that she was friendly with the author, Christina Fleischman of 18A Mansion Flats, Kensington, London SW7 9NY, for a number of years and that they recently quarrelled. Christina claimed that she would 'get back' at your client after this argument.

Your client is very upset and has been the subject of a lot of speculation as to whether the character in the book is based on her or not. She lost a role in a film which carried a fee of £5,000,000 because the producers said they were concerned that the speculation surrounding the book would detract from the film, a serious work in which Miss Bugler would have played a nun.

You have taken counsel's opinion and your barrister, Generys Hughes of Little Court Chambers, London W1D 4TX, whom you have retained in the event that the case goes to court, thinks you have a good case in light of recent controversy over alleged eating disorders. You decide to issue proceedings against the author and the publishers.

Using the multiple choice questions which follow, draft the particulars of claim for this matter.

In this exercise, you will be given a choice of clauses to put into the particulars of claim. Answer the questions below to choose the clauses that you feel are most appropriate. By answering the questions below, you will 'build' your particulars of claim. You can preview your particulars of claim at any stage, by clicking on the 'Preview your document' button after each question or on the 'Document' tab. When you are happy with your answers, click 'submit'. Your feedback and score will be presented on the 'Document' screen.

| Questions | Document |

1) Complete the details of the parties to the action.

○ Claimant Matilda Bugler

and

(1) Christina Fleischman

Defendants

(2) Grumbly Grossmere Limited

○ Claimant Matilda Bugler

and

(1) Grumbly Grossmere Limited

If you change something in a precedent or add a clause, you will need to check that this does not necessitate further amendments elsewhere in the document. A simple example is where your precedent refers, for example, to 'lessees' and you have a single lessee. In electronic documents this is usually relatively straightforward and can be done with a 'search and replace' function (although it is strongly recommended that you check each one as you go, rather than simply clicking on 'replace all').

If you insert a new term, for example, if you have a guarantor in your lease and the precedent does not refer to a guarantor, you will need to think about where the term should be inserted. In some cases, including a new term in a definition will be enough to include it everywhere in the document. Instead of adding the phrase 'and the guarantor' to 'the parties' several times in your document, you could amend the definition of 'the parties' so that it includes 'the guarantor'. This will minimize the amendments that you need to make.

You should also delete words, phrases or even entire clauses if they are not appropriate for your client's situation. For example, if there are several clauses in your lease dealing with car parking and there are no car parking facilities included in the lease, delete the clauses. Remember that if you delete clauses, you will need to check the clause numbering so that you do not have anomalies such as clause 16 being immediately followed by clause 25.

4.3.3 Boilerplates

Boilerplates are ready drafted clauses for inclusion in your document. There will be a number of standard clauses which can be included in your basic draft to cover commonly used clauses such as choice of law, when the parties are deemed to have received notices sent in the post and so on. The same rules regarding the adaptation of precedents apply to boilerplate clauses. They may be suitable as they are, but you should always consider whether they work with your document and your client's situation and adapt them accordingly.

If you are using your firm's precedent, generally they will have a number of boilerplate clauses that you can use. The advantage of obtaining all your drafting resources from a single place is that the tone and style should be similar and can therefore be amended from the point of view of suiting the facts.

4.3.4 House style

Your firm will have its own house style as to how documents should be drafted. This will cover not only issues such as the style of a document, but also other matters such as how text is to be divided. It may seem a small point, but how the text is set up can have implications for cross-referencing and interpretation throughout the document.

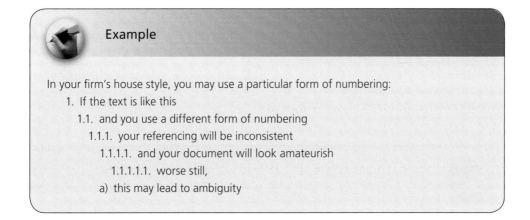

In many cases, automatic paragraph numbering will be in use and will default to your firm's house style. If this is the case, you will need to ensure that you group your text together appropriately and in the way that you meant.

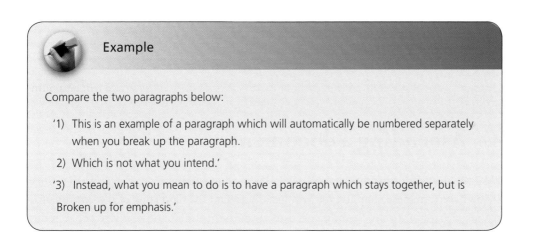

Check how your text looks as you draft. Your aim is to ensure that it is set out as you intended, conveying your meaning clearly and in compliance with your firm's house style. Your firm will have precedents which you can adapt for your client's needs and these will automatically be in house style. In some cases, however, you may need to adapt an external precedent such as:

- Suggested wording from the SRA, dealing with issues such as money laundering

- Wording or forms from HM Revenue & Customs, for example for some types of employee share schemes

- A precedent from the *Encyclopaedia of Forms and Precedents* or *Kelly's Draftsman*

In each case, you will need to adapt the precedent and ensure that it is in house style before passing it to your supervisor. If your drafting is sound, but your document is full of small points in which it is inconsistent with house style, the overall impression will be unfavourable. If the document is in house style, the quality of your drafting will be more apparent, allowing you a chance to impress.

Summary Points

■ NEVER simply use a precedent (especially not one from another file) without amending it first

■ If your firm has precedents which would be suitable for your client's matter, use them in preference to commercial precedents to ensure they are in house style

■ Do not be afraid to delete things that do not apply, but be careful not to delete anything essential in error when you do so

■ Use house style for your documents and adapt any precedents that are not in house style

---

4.4 Amending a document

How you deal with amendments will depend in part on what support you have as a trainee. If you have secretarial support, you will usually amend the hard copy of the document in manuscript, (ie write any amendments directly onto the draft), and pass it to the secretary to make the amendments.

If you do not have secretarial support, you may still wish to consider amending in manuscript and then putting the amendments into the document on your computer. One reason for this is that you then have a mechanism for checking your amendments once they are made. Also, it is still generally the case that most people find proofreading a hard copy of a document easier than reading it on screen and will pick up more points in this way. In addition, if you are interrupted, it is not usually regarded as good practice to leave a document open on your screen. It may cause your computer to crash, pose a confidentiality risk if the document is sensitive and may also prevent colleagues from making their amendments if the draft is transactional (see below).

It is very easy to lose track of where you had got to in the document, although this can be addressed to some extent by using 'red line and strikeout', a method of tracking changes to the document on screen. Whether your firm uses this will be a matter of policy for each firm and sometimes for each department or even fee-earner. Check if you should use it if you are not sure. Most firms make some use of this function, so it would be useful to ensure that you know how to use it. Use the 'Help' function so that you do not waste time trying to work out how to use it effectively.

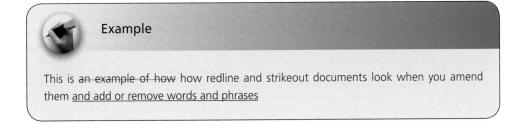

Example

This is ~~an example of how~~ how redline and strikeout documents look when you amend them <u>and add or remove words and phrases</u>

The changes can be made permanent when they are agreed and the draft will then show the amended version without the markings.

4.4.1 Transactional drafting

Much of the drafting that you do will have a transactional element. For example, you may be involved in drafting documents relating to the sale and purchase of real property, business interests, shares and so on. There is, in most situations, a generally accepted order as to who is to draft which documents. You will be on different 'sides', ie for seller in one deal, buyer in another, so you will frequently be dealing with documentation which has been drafted by other solicitors from firms whose house style and precedents are different from those in your firm. You would not, in this case, spend time converting the document into your house style. What you would do is to amend a document drafted by a third party to protect your client.

Amending a document in these circumstances depends on a number of factors. Unless your client is in a very strong position, you will not be able to arrive at a draft that gives your client everything that they could possibly want. Broadly, clauses in a document drafted by the solicitors for the other party to the transaction will fall into a number of categories:

- Entirely acceptable to your client – leave in and make no amendment
- Neutral – probably no need to amend, but see below
- Inconsistent – for example, in an international agreement, a clause has been added by the other side about which country's law is to be used to resolve disputes; the clause is not consistent with your agreement in negotiations and you would therefore amend it

- Correction of errors – for example, the name of your client's company is wrong
- To your client's disadvantage:

    — If the clause is not a 'deal breaker' or especially disadvantageous, amend it but be aware that you may have to be prepared to concede and allow the clause depending on how negotiations proceed (see below)
    — If the clause is unacceptable, you would always seek to amend but may have to concede it if your client is in a weaker position or is very keen that the deal should go ahead

4.4.2 Negotiating amendments

Part of the skill in transactional drafting is negotiating the amendments. You will develop this skill during your training contract, but broadly it involves you making a judgement about whether a clause can be conceded (ie you agree not to make your amendment) without damaging your client's position. Often, where the issue is significant, you will have to take your client's instructions.

In some cases, you will have to concede smaller points in order to secure larger ones. In any negotiation, both sides should feel that they have won. You may therefore have to add tactical amendments to your list of drafting skills, making amendments that you feel fairly certain you will have to concede in order to have something to offer the other side in exchange for the points you really mind about.

Transactional drafting used to be carried out using a 'travelling draft' which each side amended and sent back to the other. There were conventions about what colour ink was to be used to make which level of amendment so that the party who had made the amendment and the timing of the amendments could be readily identified. Now that most drafts are created and amended on a computer and passed between the parties, in many cases by email, these conventions are rarely used. Instead, many firms make electronic amendments using red line and strikeout to mark up the document electronically.

How the interim stages of drafting are recorded will depend on your firm's policy. For example, some firms will print out hard copy of a draft at various stages and retain them in a file. Other firms will save electronic versions of the different drafts in a file on their system. How your firm deals with this issue should be fairly obvious, but if in doubt, ask.

When the final version of a transactional document is agreed, a signature copy is prepared, often on higher-quality paper than draft versions. This is called an engrossment. Engrossments are also prepared for wills and litigation matters, once the final version is agreed. Wills and litigation documents were often sewn with legal tape (green for non-contentious, pink for contentious), but heat and spiral binding have taken over from this practice in the majority of firms.

It is also common practice to print off the final version on ordinary paper for proofreading before it goes into its final version. This should pick up any small typographical errors, spelling, grammar and cross-referencing points and ensure that the document is correct. Often a trainee will be involved in this time-consuming but important exercise. This is because you will have a fuller understanding of the implications of small errors. You are therefore more likely to pick up inconsistencies, where administrative staff might only pick up the errors relating to the production of the document, such as typographical errors.

> ### Summary Points
>
> - Amending draft documents is an important part of transactional work
> - Amendments need to take into account your client's standpoint
> - Some amendments may have to be conceded to secure others which matter more to your client
> - Red line and strikeout are helpful in marking up documents for amendment
> - Proofreading is an essential exercise as it requires an understanding of the law, your client's perspective and what has been negotiated

4.5 Cross-references

We have already briefly considered the issue of referencing in a document. In virtually every document, you will need to refer to other parts of the document in some of the clauses you draft. For example, if you are drafting a clause about how the tax on a particular point should be dealt with, you will usually want to refer to what happens in the event of a dispute between the parties. If there is already a clause in your document that deals with disputes, it is easier to simply refer to it, rather than reproducing the provisions again in the clause dealing with tax. Most of your drafting exercises will include cross-referencing.

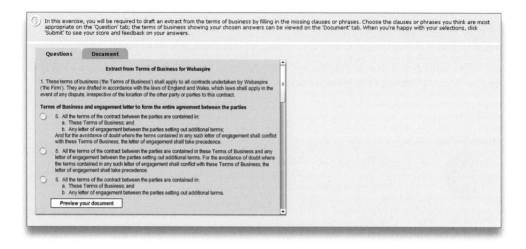

Part of the proofreading process involves checking that all the cross-references are effective and that the addition of any clauses has been taken into account in the cross-referencing. The addition of a clause can mean a change to the numbering of the clauses that come after it. This will have to be taken into account when checking any existing cross-references and adding new ones. This may seem a small point, and it is not often that this leads to ambiguity, but it makes your document look amateurish and can give clients the impression that you do not know what you are doing.

4.5.1 Consistency and contradiction

Where you are amending a document drafted by another firm, any clause that you wish to insert into the document to address an issue that is significant for your client needs to be drawn up so that it will work with the rest of the document. You will also need to ensure that your definitions are consistent with those already in the document (see 4.2.1 above). If you wish to use a term in a way that is slightly different to the existing definition, you will need to introduce a new definition which can be distinguished from the existing one.

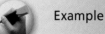

Example

If your document refers to the property known as Flat 21, 46 Arcadia Avenue London W1 4RF ('the Property'), and you wish to insert a clause about Flat 22 at the same address, you will need to have a different definition for Flat 22 (possibly 'the Second Property'). You will need to ensure when you check your document that both definitions are used consistently and do not get confused.

4.5.2 Linking documents together

In some cases, you will use more than one document to accomplish a single purpose. For example, acquisition agreements for the sale of companies are usually accompanied by documents dealing with the tax issues. These are often contained in separate documents. When drafting a will, any codicil (document amending the will) to that will is contained in a separate document.

When there is more than one document in a transaction or when one document amends another, each document must be linked to the other as far as possible. This is usually achieved by drafting each document so that it refers to the others.

This will not, of course, be possible where there is a single document and a later one is used to amend it, as would be the case with a codicil. In this case, the later document must refer to the earlier and make it clear that it is intended to amend the earlier document. In the case of a codicil drafted by the solicitor who holds the original will, the documents should be held together so that it will be apparent that they should be read together on the death of the person whose wishes they contain.

Summary Points

■ Cross-refer to other clauses in your document, rather than repeating information

■ If you insert or amend information, check that it is consistent with the rest of the document and amend where appropriate

■ Where you are using more than one document for the same matter, ensure that they refer to each other where appropriate

---

4.6 A word about completing forms

Completing forms is a frequent duty for solicitors, depending on their area of practice. Your experience on the LPC will tell you that this is not as easy as it looks. It is important to ensure that the forms you complete are entirely correct so far as you can make them. If they contain errors or inconsistencies, they are likely to be rejected or to cause you or a colleague to waste time having to redo them or to address the queries raised.

Which forms you routinely complete will depend on the type of work you are doing at the time. In company commercial work, you will complete Companies House forms and tax forms (for example when stamping a transfer of shares). In property work, you will have a substantial number of forms to complete to transfer the property and to register that transfer, plus searches and enquiries. In probate work, there are numerous forms to complete to obtain a grant which allows you to administer the estate, tax returns for the estate and the deceased and so on.

In some firms, these forms will be automatically completed by a case management system, which allows you to enter all relevant information once and leaves the completion of the forms to the system to some extent. In this case remember the RIRO principle. This stands for 'rubbish in, rubbish out'. Essentially, the form that is filled in by a system is only as good as the data that you provided to the system. If the data is inaccurate, the form will be inaccurate. Careful proofreading should pick up errors in factual information, such as misspelled names and incorrect addresses.

If you can complete forms electronically, this is usually preferable to handwriting them as it is far easier to correct any mistakes and ensures that your form is legible. Many forms are available electronically, including many that are available over the internet, from HM Revenue & Customs website, the Lord Chancellor's website and so on. You will get a good idea of how your firm does things quite quickly. If your firm uses a package like Laserforms^{TM}, you would usually receive some training on that package if you have not used it during your LPC. Online, the case study exercises include an example of completing a form on behalf of your client.

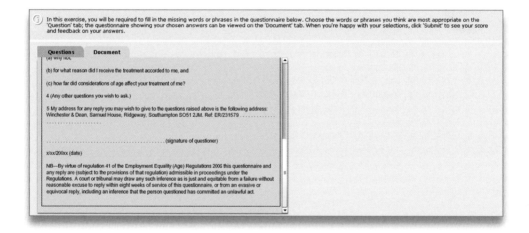

Essential Principles

There are some fairly obvious rules about completing forms which can speed up the completion process and minimize the amount of time you will have to spend revising the form once it is completed.

- Ensure that you have the correct form before you start. Some processes will have a number of forms which accomplish the same things, but which are used in different circumstances. For example, when acting for a deceased person, the oath you will need to complete to apply for a grant of representation will be different depending on whether there was a will and whether there are executors

- If there are any explanatory notes, read them before you start to draft. Often forms will have general points at the beginning of the notes (if there are any) and then notes for particular clauses. It is probably easiest to read the general notes first and then the notes for each clause as you come to it

- Assemble any information you will need to complete the form before you begin. It will be much quicker to draft in this way than to have to keep stopping, finding the information you want and then starting again

- When you have completed the form, check it thoroughly and amend if necessary. Some people find that the first few times they draft a new form, it is helpful to print it off and tick each item as it is verified. This may be particularly useful if your form contains calculations or lots of figures taken from other documents

The most important point about forms is not to underestimate them. Filling out forms is simply drafting within a very tight framework and requires knowledge and understanding of the purpose and context of the form in the same way as drafting any other type of document.

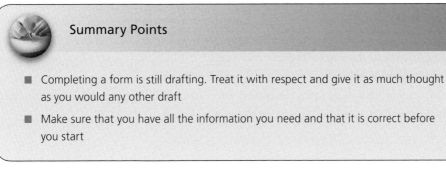

Summary Points

- ■ Completing a form is still drafting. Treat it with respect and give it as much thought as you would any other draft
- ■ Make sure that you have all the information you need and that it is correct before you start

4.7 The exercises

There are a number of drafting exercises in the writing and drafting part of your online resource. Some of them have already been mentioned in the text above. They include exercises using multiple choice questions to provide you with alternatives for clauses that are used to draft documents in a number of scenarios. Missing word and true/false exercises are also used to give you an idea of the process of drafting. In many cases, there will be more than one right answer and indeed some answers that are partially correct and will receive credit. Drafting is not an exact science and issues of tone, consistency and clarity matter just as much in drafting as they do in writing.

The exercises for drafting are towards the end of the writing and drafting module as the basic principles of writing apply equally to drafting. As you will see from the 'map' set out in the writing section, you will be asked to draft in the context of all of your compulsory subjects, to help give you a broad experience of this skill.

4.7.1 How to approach this module

Read the writing section if you have not already done so. Your tutor may give you guidance as to when you should read the relevant section and complete the exercises. You will need to complete the writing exercises first as the nature of the package means that they need to be done in the order set out in pathways for each skill area. As with the writing part of this module, some exercises will have supplementary exercises which you can attempt if you score less than 50% on the original exercise. If you achieve less than 50% on the supplementary exercises, you are strongly advised to speak to your tutor.

4.8 Conclusions

As with any legal (or non-legal) skill, it is practice that has the biggest effect on how you perform in tasks in which that skill is used. Making use of the feedback you receive in the exercises in this module should help support you in your training contract so that your drafting enables you to demonstrate that you are capable and can produce high-quality drafting. If you can show in early drafts that you are competent, you are likely to be trusted with more substantial pieces of drafting. This will mean that you will gain more experience and that your work will be more interesting and varied, making your training more effective and richer than would otherwise be the case.

www.**oxford**interact.com

Introduction

Reflective Learning

Legal Writing

Drafting

■ **Interviewing and Advising**

Advocacy

Practical Legal Research

Section 5

Interviewing and Advising

Introduction

Interviewing is a skill which has a rather wider application than simply interviewing clients. The object of interviewing is to determine what it is that your client wants or needs from you and to get enough information to enable you to help them. It also transfers to other contexts too. For example, if your supervisor gives you a piece of work to do, asking questions about what they require and additional information you need to achieve that, this is a form of interviewing.

The other aspect of the skill is advising. Clearly this involves a sound knowledge of the law, but it also involves being able to explain the issue to the client so that they will understand, but without descending into patronizing them or oversimplifying.

Because this skill involves direct contact with clients, you will need to ensure that you conduct yourself professionally. If you do not achieve this, your client may decide that they do not wish to instruct you or, if they do, they will be anxious about whether or not you know what you are doing. If they do not have confidence in you, they may insist on calling you far more than is necessary, running up costs and leading to a larger bill, which they are then more likely to dispute!

There are various ways that you can practise this skill. During your LPC, find out if your provider has a *pro bono* scheme. Getting involved in this type of work is helpful for your skill development and will usually impress a prospective employer. It also provides you with a great opportunity to practise your skills, not to mention that you are also helping others!

The SRA's written standards

The standards for interviewing and advising and all other areas of the LPC are available from the SRA website (www.sra.org.uk).

5.1 The Interviewing module

The 'map' set out below shows the structure of the interviewing online course. When you go online, you can check the 'What's new?' section to see if any new exercises have been added. The online course includes supplementary exercises (shaded blue on the map below) which you will be prompted to complete before proceeding to the next exercise in the event that you achieve less than 50% of the marks in the main exercise. Having completed the supplementary exercise, you should then move on to the next exercise.

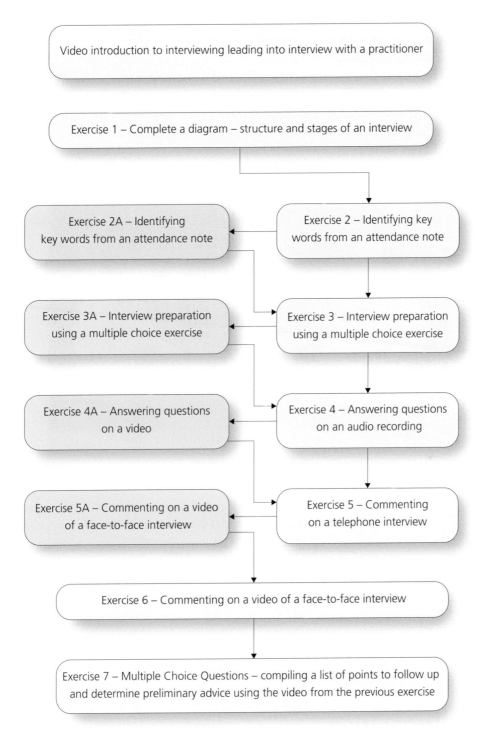

Video introduction to interviewing leading into interview with a practitioner

Exercise 1 – Complete a diagram – structure and stages of an interview

Exercise 2A – Identifying key words from an attendance note

Exercise 2 – Identifying key words from an attendance note

Exercise 3A – Interview preparation using a multiple choice exercise

Exercise 3 – Interview preparation using a multiple choice exercise

Exercise 4A – Answering questions on a video

Exercise 4 – Answering questions on an audio recording

Exercise 5A – Commenting on a video of a face-to-face interview

Exercise 5 – Commenting on a telephone interview

Exercise 6 – Commenting on a video of a face-to-face interview

Exercise 7 – Multiple Choice Questions – compiling a list of points to follow up and determine preliminary advice using the video from the previous exercise

The exercises cover the issues in this section, including preparation, selecting keywords to assist with advising and follow-up as well as the conduct of the interview itself. The exercises also include explaining legal issues to clients using information provided. There are seven exercises, plus four back-up exercises. There is no time limit on any of the exercises, although they will have to be done in order.

In the case study exercises, the client interview is the first part of the extended case study and you will make use of the information from the first interview in the subsequent parts of the case study.

The module focuses on the skill of interviewing and takes you through various scenarios to help you get a good idea of what is needed to master this skill. There is some general guidance on LPC assessments in the introductory section. Broadly, as with any other skill assessment, you should ensure that you review any guidance on the form of your assessment and the criteria which will be used to assess you. You should consider how you can meet those criteria. If you have concerns about your performance in this or any skill, you should discuss them with a tutor at an early stage. Any mock or practice sessions, as well as the interactive exercises, should be used to consider how you can improve your skills and meet the necessary criteria to pass your assessment.

5.2 Preparation

Every interview, like every client, is different. However, unless the client turns up unexpectedly, or your work is such that you can be called in to deal with a matter at very short notice, as may happen in, for example, criminal work if you are on call, you will always need to prepare for the interview with the client. Failing to prepare will mean that you may ask questions for which the client may feel you should already have answers. You may also stumble on legal issues and are likely to come across as unprofessional.

5.2.1 Practical issues

Your firm will have its own procedures for opening files for new clients and new matters for existing clients. You should find out what these are and follow them when dealing with new matters.

If the client is new to the firm, you will need to consider professional conduct issues such as conflict checks (to ensure that you are able to act for the client) and money laundering. The Money Laundering Regulations require that in many cases, the identity of a new client is checked by the solicitor. In many cases, you will need to ask a client to bring evidence of their identity (usually two forms are required) to your meeting so that you can check it and record it on their file. Part of your preparation is therefore likely to involve informing the client that this will happen and explaining why. Exercise 3 looks at preparation for an interview and the writing and drafting exercises give examples of the type of letter you might send out to a client covering the issues considered in this section.

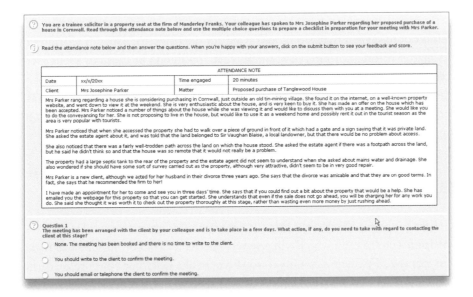

If your client has not been to your office before, you will need to ensure that they know how to get to you and where to park if they are arriving by car. Most firms will have maps or directions for clients and there will usually be a procedure for booking a parking space. This may seem like a small point, but if you have told the client that they can park in the firm's car park and this is not possible, they will be annoyed and frustrated and the interview is unlikely to go well!

The timing of the client care letter will depend on your firm's normal practice. If you are sending out a client care letter (sometimes called an engagement letter) before the interview, you can include information about parking, directions etc as an enclosure, along with your terms of business and any other relevant information. You will also need to include details about issues such as costs, complaints procedures and other information which the SRA requires solicitors to provide to their clients. You will cover this in more detail in the professional conduct part of your LPC.

5.2.2 Legal issues

If you have been able to identify any legal issues from the initial contact with your client, you may wish to consider any points arising before the interview. Approach this with caution. Part of the initial interview involves determining the legal issues and your client's objectives. If the client has told you a significant amount about their matter on the initial contact and you feel you can usefully check before the interview, it is clearly beneficial to do this. However, what you will need to avoid is spending too much time on what may turn out to be a 'blind alley' either because the client has not really given you enough information, or because the information provided has given you the wrong impression as to the issue. Most firms charge their clients on the basis of the time spent on their matter and the time of those working on the file is recorded so that it can be billed. If the time does turn out to be wasted, you will not be able to bill it and it will have to be written off.

This is not to suggest that you should avoid considering legal issues in relation to your client's matter before your interview, simply that you should be cautious about spending large amounts of time looking into what the client *might* be going to consult you about. If you know definitely what it is about, time spent preparing beforehand will be invaluable preparation, but consider whether you know enough to do a significant amount without wasting time.

5.2.3 The client's history

If the client has been a client of the firm for some time, it is generally useful to review information from a previous file which will give you a better idea of how to approach their matter. For example, if a client is coming to you because of a neighbour dispute, an earlier file on a similar matter is likely to be helpful to you. Earlier files will certainly provide you with information regarding full name, address and other details, although you should confirm any details with the client. They may have moved house or changed job, the partnership might have incorporated and now be run as a company and so on. If you ask the client 'are you still at 27 Ridgeway Road?' rather than, 'Can you give me your address, please?', this tells the client that you have taken the trouble to find out about them and will give them confidence in you. Be careful, however. If they tell you that they moved six years ago and your firm did the conveyancing, this will not create the impression that you want!

Essential Principles

You should, if you can, try to prepare for your interview in the same way as you would for any other interview, by finding out as much as you can about the client beforehand. In addition to reviewing their files if there are any, if they are a business client, see if they have a website that you can check so that you can get some idea of their background. If they are a new, individual client, this will obviously be very difficult, but if there are sources of information about your client, use them to help you.

5.2.4 The client's matter

When you are interviewing the client, you should expect them to do most of the talking. You need to find out:

- The facts (part of your skill as a lawyer involves determining which facts are the most important/relevant and which are less so)

- The legal issues (these should become apparent from the facts, although bear in mind that some legal issues may not become clear until you have started to research them later)

- What your client wants to achieve (the end result). In some cases, what the client wants and what is possible will not marry up – in a criminal matter, for example, the client will usually want to get out of the police station as soon as possible!

- What is their attitude to risk (what are they prepared to do to achieve that result and how would they prefer to go about it?)

- Any limitations (do they have a financial or time limit for achieving their end result?)

- Any factors that might affect your advice

You should be wary of trying to control the interview too tightly, although you need to ensure that it does not become rambling and irrelevant. It can sometimes be difficult to judge whether the client is going off the point, or whether they are filling you in on secondary facts that are still important. Generally, the best way to deal with the client either 'drying up' or giving you information which appears to be irrelevant to the matter is to ask them a question. This needs to be done carefully. Asking 'Why is this relevant?' is likely to be regarded as offensive, but 'I'm sorry, could you clarify how that relates to the events of the 18th of February?' is less likely to be taken amiss and may help get things back on track. If the client was actually coming to the connection, it may help pull things together for you.

Essential Principles

Your manner in the interview should be professional, but not overbearing or intimidating. You want the client to feel that they have come to the right person, that you can help them, not that they are wasting your time and should look elsewhere.

Exercises 5 and 6 involve reviewing the performance of a trainee conducting an interview. When commenting on their performances in the exercises, you should bear in mind the issues raised in this section.

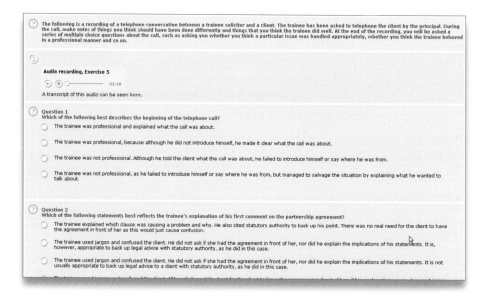

The following is a recording of a telephone conversation between a trainee solicitor and a client. The trainee has been asked to telephone the client by the principal. During the call, make notes of things you think should have been done differently and things that you think the trainee did well. At the end of the recording, you will be asked a series of multiple choice questions about the call, such as asking you whether you think a particular issue was handled appropriately, whether you think the trainee behaved in a professional manner and so on.

Audio recording, Exercise 5

02:28

A transcript of this audio can be seen here.

Question 1
Which of the following best describes the beginning of the telephone call?

○ The trainee was professional and explained what the call was about.

○ The trainee was professional, because although he did not introduce himself, he made it clear what the call was about.

○ The trainee was not professional. Although he told the client what the call was about, he failed to introduce himself or say where he was from.

○ The trainee was not professional, as he failed to introduce himself or say where he was from, but managed to salvage the situation by explaining what he wanted to talk about.

Question 2
Which of the following statements best reflects the trainee's explanation of his first comment on the partnership agreement?

○ The trainee explained which clause was causing a problem and why. He also cited statutory authority to back up his point. There was no real need for the client to have the agreement in front of her as this would just cause confusion.

○ The trainee used jargon and confused the client. He did not ask if she had the agreement in front of her, nor did he explain the implications of his statements. It is, however, appropriate to back up legal advice with statutory authority, as he did in this case.

○ The trainee used jargon and confused the client. He did not ask if she had the agreement in front of her, nor did he explain the implications of his statements. It is not usually appropriate to back up legal advice to a client with statutory authority, as he did in this case.

00:25 06:00

You also do not want the client to feel that they are being interrogated. Asking a long series of closed questions (see below) can make the client feel intimidated and as though they are being judged. Asking questions is useful, but they need to be the right kind of questions. As is considered in more detail below, open questions (those which encourage the client to explain things in their own words), are far more useful than those which can be answered in one word or just elicit a single fact.

Your client should feel that you have listened to them and understand their matter. Listening is not the same as remaining silent until it is your turn to speak. You need to make sure that you listen and understand what is being said and the client knows that you have really listened to them.

5.2.5 Open and closed questions

This is a subject which will be considered again in more detail in the advocacy section and exercises. Essentially, there are two main types of questions, open and closed. A closed question is one which can be answered very succinctly, either because it requires a yes or no answer, or because it is asking for a particular fact.

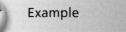

Example

'Did you see James Parks on Cornmarket Street last Saturday afternoon at 4 pm?' can usually only be answered with a confirmation or a denial. On the other hand 'Please tell me what happened last Saturday afternoon' is an open question. It invites the person answering the question to tell you, in their own words, what happened last Saturday afternoon.

It is not necessarily the case that one type of question is good and the other bad. It is more a question of using the right type to suit your purpose. If all you want is a yes or no answer, a closed question is fine. If, on the other hand, you want the client to tell you what happened so that you can build up a picture of events and understand the issue, an open question will be more effective for this purpose.

Closed questions can be very useful for checking facts such as times, dates, places, names and addresses and so on. However, in terms of the tone of the interview, asking your client a series of closed questions will, as we have considered, make them feel as though they are being interrogated and are not being given a chance to be heard. This can also come across as rather intimidating and unpleasant.

In general, it is best to use a combination of these types of question. Open questions can help the client explain what the problem is as they see it and to give you the facts. You can then check those facts ('Did you say it was James Parks you saw or Andrew Parks?') and ask supplementary questions. For example, an open question, 'What happened last Saturday afternoon?' invites them to explain how they were on Cornmarket Street shopping and they saw James Parks, while a closed question, 'Did James have a black eye?' will enable you to establish that in fact it was Andrew Parks, James' twin, and not James because James does not have a black eye.

Remember that although the client may feel that they have told you everything you need to know, there may be factors that would affect their legal position and these will obviously affect your advice. For example, if you are dealing with an intestacy and the client tells you that the deceased has a nephew, it matters whether he is a nephew by marriage, or is a nephew because he is a child of the deceased's brother or sister. In the former case, the nephew has no claim against the estate, in the latter, he may have a claim, depending on which other relatives have also survived the deceased.

It is usually better to try and avoid asking too many questions while the client is outlining their situation as this can be off-putting for them. However, if you want to clarify a point or encourage the client to expand on a key point, asking a question is generally appropriate.

Summary Points

- Ensure that you prepare for your interview – consider practical issues as well as legal

- If your firm has acted for the client before, consider reviewing the files to give you a better idea of how to deal with the client's matter

- Consider what you need to ask the client at interview – a mixture of open and closed questions will probably be most effective

- Balance the need to review the law and undertake research with the need to avoid spending too much time on issues which might not be relevant. Use your judgement

---

5.3 Conducting the interview

It may seem obvious, but ensure that you arrive on time if at all possible. A few minutes spent on a phone call after you know the client has arrived may seem to pass very quickly to you, but will seem much longer to your client who is expecting you to arrive on time. If a delay is unavoidable, ensure that the client is given a message, and apologize when you do arrive. They are more likely to accept a reasonable explanation if they are told what is happening at as early a stage as possible. For example, exercise 6 looks at how you might deal with unavoidable lateness.

00:01 06:00

5.3.1 Beginning the interview

If you have booked a meeting room, take your client to that room if they have not already been taken there by a member of the support team. It is usually polite to offer a drink – you will find out very quickly how this works at your firm. If you are meeting a client in your office, it is usually a good idea to ensure that it is reasonably presentable. You may be busy, but if there are files on every available space and papers all over your desk, it might be better to use a neutral space like a meeting room. This is definitely a good idea if you share an office.

When you greet the client, it is generally polite to shake hands. It usually creates a bad impression if your handshake is very weak and limp. However, any handshake which is so firm that you make the client feel as though you are crushing their hand is not a good idea either.

5.3.2 Tone

The tone of the interview is important in the same way that the tone of your writing is important. You need to be professional, but not intimidating or mechanical. Remember that although you will often be dealing with people who are in business, in many areas of legal work you are dealing with people who are upset and you will need to use a certain amount of tact. For example, in a private client seat, you may be dealing with someone who has suffered a recent bereavement and needs you to help them deal with the estate. They will not necessarily appreciate a brisk and efficient approach. If you are conducting crim-inal work, you may be dealing with someone who has been arrested and is possibly feeling frightened or angry. In family law, you would be dealing with issues such as divorce and child welfare, both of which are very emotional for the clients concerned.

You will need to bear all this in mind and be careful about how you conduct the interview, particularly if the client is very emotional. For example, if you are interviewing a client who is recently bereaved, referring to their late father as 'the deceased', although technically correct, comes across as inhumane.

Be careful to remain reasonably detached in an emotionally charged situation. For example, if your client is about to undertake litigation, they may be feeling angry and aggrieved.

 Essential Principles

You need to stand back from the situation and give your client sound advice. If their case is unfair, but has no legal cause of action, they need to be told that that is the case. Equally, someone who is bereaved or going through a traumatic experience may regard you as a shoulder to cry on. You need to walk a very fine line between being sensitive to your client and remaining professional.

5.3.3 Body language

There is now little dispute that the unconscious signals given by body language do matter and should be considered. Generally, when interviewing a client, try to establish and maintain eye contact in a natural way, rather than with a fixed, hawkish stare. This is difficult to do if you are trying to write every word your client says, hence the later suggestions about brief notes and mind maps. Self-conscious 'listening poses' will look unnatural and you will probably be focusing on maintaining the impression, rather than what the client is actually saying.

What you are aiming to do is to make the client feel at ease, so that they will be able to explain their matter to you. You also want to build up a rapport, which you will not do if you avoid eye contact and generally act in an aloof manner, or make them feel that you are not listening.

Simple things like saying 'I see' or nodding at various intervals can encourage your client, although again, the focus needs to be on what the client is saying. You should be focusing on listening to what is being said, not on timing yourself to say something encouraging every 30 seconds. If you are genuinely listening to the client, giving them your full attention, you will almost certainly do this naturally anyway.

Essential Principles

Beware of using slang or unbusinesslike expressions in this context. If your client tells you something which really helps your case, using the sort of slang expression you might use among your friends is not likely to go down well!

Small things like how you greet the client, your demeanour and how you conduct yourself can be very important in establishing a rapport and making the client feel that you are someone they can trust. You are aiming to create a professional impression.

During your interviewing course, you will probably be recorded at least once. Do make sure that you watch the tapes as they can really help in understanding how you appear to others. Small things like spinning or clicking with your pen can be really distracting and, more importantly, give the client the impression that you are bored and not listening to them. Other gestures such as leaning back with your hands behind your head when thinking or folding your arms can give the client the feeling that you do not believe them or that you are not taking them seriously.

5.3.4 Phone calls

Unless you are expecting an urgent call (in which case you should warn your client and explain that you might receive a call and why it is urgent), switch off your mobile if you have it with you. The circumstances would have to be very unusual indeed for you to take a call during your interview. The client is likely to feel that they are less important than your call and may have second thoughts about whether they wish to instruct you.

5.3.5 Professional conduct

There are various professional conduct issues that will need to be considered as part of your interview. Some conduct issues will have been covered already in your client care letter, although you should be prepared to check that your client understands the information in relation to costs in particular. Confidentiality is critical to the solicitor/client relationship and is a key principle of professional conduct. You should ensure that the client knows that what they tell you is confidential as this may encourage the client to be open and frank with you. You may also have to address issues such as ensuring that you take instructions from your client, not a third party, for example, if a well-meaning friend or relative comes along to help your elderly client give instructions for a will. You will cover confidentiality more fully in your professional conduct module.

5.3.6 The time factor

There are very few firms which do not charge according to time spent on a client's matter. Many firms offer an initial interview without charge, but this will often be limited to half an hour. Be guided by your firm's policy. Generally however, time is important and you will need to balance the need to offer the client a good service with constraints on your time. You do not want to have to cut the client off in mid-sentence when their time is up, but nor do you want to have to write off hours of time for which you cannot charge.

This is an issue which you will have to handle carefully and with some tact. The client's expectations should be managed and, if appropriate, you need to convey to them that you want to be thorough, but not to cause their costs to escalate. The client care letter will advise your client of your charge-out rate and give an estimate of your likely costs, which should help you to address this issue with your client. Exercise 5A gives an example of the issue of reminding a client that the costs are charged on a time basis and also on how this information is delivered.

Some firms charge a fixed or agreed fee in some matters, rather than charging according to the time spent. Your firm will advise you if they carry out work on this basis and how it is to be charged if they do so. For example, many firms will charge a fixed fee for incorporating a company, or drafting a simple will, but may still charge on a time basis for commercial work.

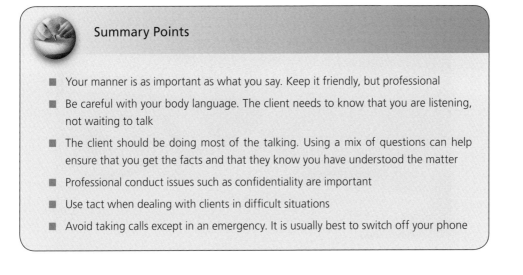

Summary Points

- Your manner is as important as what you say. Keep it friendly, but professional

- Be careful with your body language. The client needs to know that you are listening, not waiting to talk

- The client should be doing most of the talking. Using a mix of questions can help ensure that you get the facts and that they know you have understood the matter

- Professional conduct issues such as confidentiality are important

- Use tact when dealing with clients in difficult situations

- Avoid taking calls except in an emergency. It is usually best to switch off your phone

5.4 Taking notes

During the interview, you are likely to want to make some notes as your client explains the issue. Although you will want to take as full a note as you can, remember that it is difficult to get down every word while your client is still speaking. The average person speaks at an astounding 150–200 words per minute,[1] which is likely to be faster than you can record it. In addition, if you are focusing on writing, you are not focusing on the client. They are likely to be looking at the top of your head as you look down at your notes.

You will develop your own method of dealing with taking notes, but you may find that initially it is easier to jot down a few key points as the client speaks and to fill out your notes once the client has finished explaining their matter. The format that you use is, again, a matter of personal choice, but remember that the way you took notes in lectures is unlikely to work in this context. In lectures, you did not have to interact to any significant extent with the lecturer, unless they initiated this or you asked a question. In general, however, there was no real dialogue. When you are interviewing a client, the situation is different and your method of dealing with the issue of recording the interview will not necessarily be the same either.

Exercise 6 shows a trainee dealing with note-taking in an interview.

---

1 Psycholinguistics Research Group of the University of Essex, www.essex.ac.uk/psyling/eyelab.html.

Some trainees find that using a 'mind map' format, rather than writing in full sentences on lines, facilitates the record of the interview. An example is set out below.

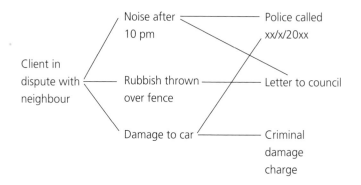

This is a very basic example, but the idea is simply to record the facts, dates, action points and so on in groups, rather than in sentences which may be separated by a number of pages of text if you had tried to write everything down. It is also easier to add extra points where they are relevant. In a situation where you are required to take brief but informative notes and maintain an engagement with the client, this may be a helpful format to use.

The same information is presented in a linear format below:

'The client is in dispute with their neighbour. There have been various incidents including noise after 10 pm on a number of occasions, damage to the client's car and rubbish thrown over the fence. The client called the police on xx/x/20xx in relation to the noise and the damage to the car. A charge of criminal damage was brought in relation to the damage to the car. The client has written to the council regarding the rubbish thrown over the fence and the noise.'

5.4.1 Checking the facts

If you have made brief notes while the client is speaking, you may wish to check the facts with them at various points during the interview and often at the end as well, to check that your overview, as well as the detail, is correct. Depending on what you have noted down and the complexity of the facts, you could either check particular facts with the client, or go through a brief summary and invite them to add or correct as appropriate.

Whichever method you use, you must ensure that you leave the meeting with notes that you are confident give you the information that you need to take things forward. If you are not certain, it is better to ask at the interview than telephone the client afterwards and give them the impression that you do not really know what you are doing.

When you are making a note of a meeting, it is usually better to dictate or type up any notes as soon after the meeting as you can. Notes that made sense to you at the time may mean nothing to you if you leave the meeting note until a week or so later.

Summary Points

- Take brief notes during the interview, but give your client your attention
- Check any key facts and important issues with the client either during or at the end of the interview

---

5.5 **Advising**

There are a number of misconceptions about how to advise clients. The most significant misconception is that a solicitor tells a client what to do. This is not really what advising is about. The solicitor will advise the client about the possible courses of action (sometimes there will only be one) and the client then makes an informed choice about how to proceed.

You should only advise a client when you have listened to the client and ensured that you have all the relevant facts. If you need to conduct research before advising, tell the client that this is the case, rather than trying to advise 'off the top of your head' and risking misleading the client or, worse still, leading them to do entirely the wrong thing.

Once you have reached a conclusion as to the legal position, you then need to ensure that you explain this to your client. Avoid using jargon or referring too much (or at all, in most cases) to legislation. Telling your client that the law says X or Y is usually enough, but be prepared to tell the client which Act or case is involved if they actually want to know. This does not mean that you should 'dumb down' the law for your client. Remember that in most cases, your client is asking you to deal with this because they do not know what the law says and need your help. Explaining the legal position clearly, without using jargon but not in a way that is patronizing or condescending will help your client to make an informed choice.

Exercises 5 and 6 address the issue of how (and how not to!) advise.

The following is a recording of a telephone conversation between a trainee solicitor and a client. The trainee has been asked to telephone the client by the principal. During the call, make notes of things you think should have been done differently and things that you think the trainee did well. At the end of the recording, you will be asked a series of multiple choice questions about the call, such as asking you whether you think a particular issue was handled appropriately, whether you think the trainee behaved in a professional manner and so on.

Audio recording, Exercise 5

02:28

A transcript of this audio can be seen here.

Question 1
Which of the following best describes the beginning of the telephone call?

○ The trainee was professional and explained what the call was about.

○ The trainee was professional, because although he did not introduce himself, he made it clear what the call was about.

○ The trainee was not professional. Although he told the client what the call was about, he failed to introduce himself or say where he was from.

○ The trainee was not professional, as he failed to introduce himself or say where he was from, but managed to salvage the situation by explaining what he wanted to talk about.

Question 2
Which of the following statements best reflects the trainee's explanation of his first comment on the partnership agreement?

○ The trainee explained which clause was causing a problem and why. He also cited statutory authority to back up his point. There was no real need for the client to have the agreement in front of her as this would just cause confusion.

○ The trainee used jargon and confused the client. He did not ask if she had the agreement in front of her, nor did he explain the implications of his statements. It is, however, appropriate to back up legal advice with statutory authority, as he did in this case.

○ The trainee used jargon and confused the client. He did not ask if she had the agreement in front of her, nor did he explain the implications of his statements. It is not usually appropriate to back up legal advice to a client with statutory authority, as he did in this case.

When advising a client about how to proceed in a matter, you need to bear in mind that there are issues other than law that will affect your client's decision about how to proceed. In a business matter, commercial factors will play a big part in how you take the matter forward for your client. In private client matters, personal and practical factors will be significant. If you noted these factors in the initial interview and formed a view on what your client was trying to achieve and the routes they were prepared to take to get there, you should be able to tailor your advice accordingly.

If the matter is contentious, your client's attitude to risk will play a big part in how they take things forward. You will need to make sure that they know and understand the implications of each possible course of action and likely moves by the other side in a dispute.

Remember that in some cases, professional conduct will also have a bearing on how you advise your client to proceed. For example, if they wish you to lie to the court on their behalf, you will have to advise them that you cannot do this and explain that if they insist you will have to cease to act.

5.5.1 Difficult questions

Clients will often ask you awkward questions to which you do not know the answer. If this happens, be honest. If you will have to undertake fairly extensive research to come to an answer, you will have to explain to the client that the point is difficult and that you will need to research this. Exercise 5 gives an example of where a client asks a trainee a question to which she doesn't know the answer.

Check with them if there is a timescale to which you need to work on the matter and agree a reasonable time to do this. Try to be realistic about how long you need. It is better to err on the side of caution and get back to them earlier than you agreed than to miss the deadline. Equally, don't try to get them to agree to deadlines that are far in excess of what you actually need to carry out the research.

If you are reasonably familiar with a point, but you think that there has been a recent change in the law, say so and tell the client that you need to check. Obviously if you have done your preparation, issues that the client raised with you before the interview should be familiar as you should have reviewed them as part of your preparation. New points that were raised at the interview are likely to be less familiar and it is usually acceptable to tell the client that you will need to check the position.

5.5.2 What if you can't help?

Rule 1 of the Code of Conduct makes it quite clear that a solicitor should not advise outside their area of knowledge. If you do not feel that you know enough to advise, you should not be trying to bluster your way through by pretending you know more than you do, although in many cases you can address this by researching the issue. It may be that you are not able to deal with their matter. For example, if the client is asking you to give advice on the suitability of investments, this is not only a possible breach of Rule 1, but you may be committing an offence. Other issues may be less dramatic – for example a client may come to you saying that they want to make a will, but actually their problem relates to pension rights as part of a divorce settlement. If you are concerned that you cannot deal with one part of the matter, or perhaps you cannot deal with the entire matter, there are various options open to you (see diagram below).

If in doubt, consult your supervisor and do not be afraid to tell a client that you do not know about a particular point. Remember that you have a duty to the court as well as to your client and exaggerating what you can do for the client by taking on work outside your knowledge does not comply with the duty to the court.

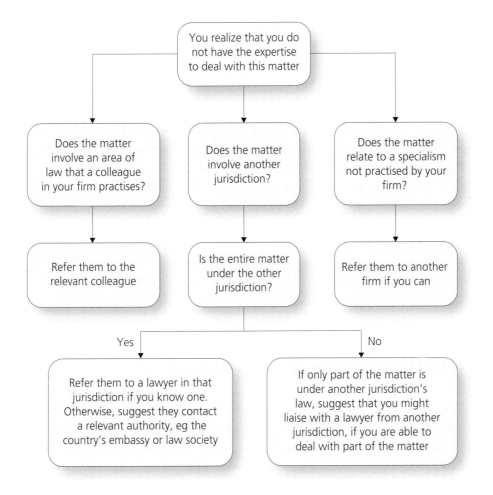

You realize that you do not have the expertise to deal with this matter

Does the matter involve an area of law that a colleague in your firm practises?

Does the matter involve another jurisdiction?

Does the matter relate to a specialism not practised by your firm?

Refer them to the relevant colleague

Is the entire matter under the other jurisdiction?

Refer them to another firm if you can

Yes

No

Refer them to a lawyer in that jurisdiction if you know one. Otherwise, suggest they contact a relevant authority, eg the country's embassy or law society

If only part of the matter is under another jurisdiction's law, suggest that you might liaise with a lawyer from another jurisdiction, if you are able to deal with part of the matter

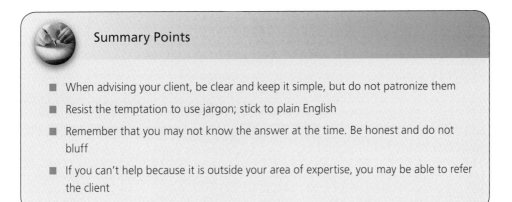

Summary Points

- When advising your client, be clear and keep it simple, but do not patronize them
- Resist the temptation to use jargon; stick to plain English
- Remember that you may not know the answer at the time. Be honest and do not bluff
- If you can't help because it is outside your area of expertise, you may be able to refer the client

5.5.3 Concluding the interview

Once you are satisfied that you have everything that you need, you can start to bring the interview to a close. Be guided by the client on this. If they have more to tell you, let them do so, rather than cutting them off because the time is up.

The client should also be satisfied that you have discussed everything that can usefully be discussed at that time and that they have made all their points. Always check with the client if there is anything else they want to mention. Sometimes last-minute points can be very valuable and can, in some cases, change everything if they are particularly significant.

Both you and the client should be clear about what is to happen next and to what timescale. If you are going to look into a particular legal point and get back to them by Wednesday of the following week, make sure that you stick to that deadline. If something unexpected happens and you realize that you cannot meet that deadline, contact the client and explain, preferably in advance, rather than waiting for the deadline to pass.

5.6 Following up the interview

Make it clear on your attendance note who is to do what and by when. If the client is to send you documents, you might want to mention this in your client care letter if you are sending one out after, rather than before, the meeting. If you have a list of things that you need to do, you might wish to write yourself a checklist and note the date next to the items as they are completed. If this is a routine matter with set tasks to undertake, some firms will have standard checklists which should be used in these matters. For example, in a conveyancing matter, there may be a checklist of searches, communications to send to the client and documents for drafting. Some firms will have case management systems to deal with this point.

Exercise 7 gives an example of a checklist which you might use to follow up an interview.

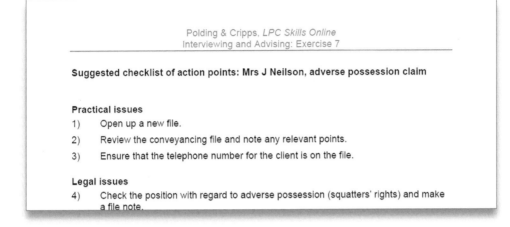

Polding & Cripps, *LPC Skills Online*
Interviewing and Advising: Exercise 7

Suggested checklist of action points: Mrs J Neilson, adverse possession claim

Practical issues
1) Open up a new file.
2) Review the conveyancing file and note any relevant points.
3) Ensure that the telephone number for the client is on the file.

Legal issues
4) Check the position with regard to adverse possession (squatters' rights) and make a file note.

You may have agreed that you will contact someone or check something on your client's behalf. If this is the case, make sure that you have all the information you need to do this and do it as soon as you can unless you have agreed that you will do something on a particular day. If what you are to do is conditional on some other factor, particularly one outside your control, make this clear. For example, 'If Mr Smith phones me by Wednesday, I will ask him about the accident and then contact Mr Jones.'

If a client has agreed to send you something, such as a copy of their contract of employment in an employment matter, agree how and when they will send this. If you have to chase, be tactful and remember that you want to have an ongoing professional relationship with this client if possible.

Carry out any research that you need to complete as soon as you can as your client needs to know their position. Telephone or write to the client with your results and advice by any agreed deadline.

With regard to the administrative aspect of the follow-up, ensure that you complete any necessary paperwork and open a file on the matter if you have not already done so. If the client wants you to communicate with them in a particular way, for example by email rather than by post, note this on their file and stick to it if you can.

5.6.1 Key words

When you are reviewing your notes, you will need to think about the areas of law involved in the matter. Sometimes it will be obvious, but in other cases you will need to consider where you will have to start when you are researching the client's problem.

Key words are those which give you an indication of where you are and where you should be going in terms of research issues. There is more detail on this point in relation to research in the practical legal research module. Key words narrow down your field of search and sharpen your focus on the major issues.

Example

Mrs Smith sent back the bicycle which she had bought by mail order. It was not suitable for mountain biking and she had been injured when using it in accordance with the manufacturer's instructions.

The key words here are *mail order*, *injured* and *suitable*.

These tell you that there are three major issues here. Firstly, Mrs Smith has been injured (tort), secondly, the goods were not suitable (consumer protection and contract) and thirdly, they were ordered by mail order, which has its own rules regarding consumer protection.

Exercise 2 gives you some practice on this issue.

The telephone attendance note below has been passed to you by a fellow trainee who is unable to see the client as they are on holiday. They have made an appointment for the client to come in and see you tomorrow. Read through the attendance note and then answer the questions below which ask you to consider which are the key words or phrases in relation to the areas of law that are relevant to your client's case. Remember that there will be key words that relate to other matters such as your client's objectives, their situation and so on, but you should only select those that relate to areas of law. Remember that you do not need to know the law in any detail as the focus is on the skill of identifying the legal issues to discuss with your client at interview.

Read the attendance note below and then answer the questions. When you're happy with your answers, click on the submit button to see your feedback and score.

ATTENDANCE NOTE

| Date | xx/x/20xx | Time engaged | 20 minutes |
| Client | Ms Louise Scobie | Matter | Immigration dispute |

Ms Scobie recently came to the UK on holiday. She is a British citizen and works as a doctor with an aid organization, based in West Africa. She is sent to wherever she is needed and so has no permanent residence.

When she arrived in the UK four days ago, she was detained as she arrived in immigration and questioned about drugs and money laundering. She and her baggage were searched and she was detained for 72 hours. She was carrying syringes and insulin in her baggage as she is diabetic. She says that the officers who searched her bags were not concerned about the syringes and did not question her further about them once she had explained. She was very upset by the experience and feels that she was unfairly treated. She wants to be compensated for this in some way.

She is also convinced that the officers who detained her were acting on a 'tip-off', as they were waiting for her when she got off the plane. She thinks that someone from a drug smuggling ring passed information to HM Revenue & Customs and the immigration authorities suggesting that she would be carrying drugs in order to draw attention away from the real drug courier. She is concerned that inaccurate information about her may be held on the databases of the UK authorities which might be passed on to the aid organization and cause her to lose her job.

Question 1
Is 'British citizen' a key phrase?
○ Yes.
○ No.

Question 2
Is 'no permanent residence' a key phrase?
○ Yes.

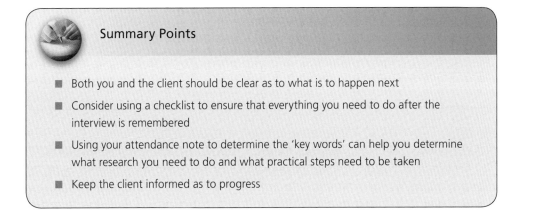

Summary Points

- Both you and the client should be clear as to what is to happen next

- Consider using a checklist to ensure that everything you need to do after the interview is remembered

- Using your attendance note to determine the 'key words' can help you determine what research you need to do and what practical steps need to be taken

- Keep the client informed as to progress

5.7 **Conclusion**

Interviewing is a key skill and the one on which much of the rest of your matter is based. If you do not obtain the information in the interview, your research will be flawed and so will your advice. You will also create a bad impression and come across as unprofessional to your client and to your firm. If you conduct your interview well, it will ensure that you have a sound foundation on which to base the rest of the conduct of the matter and you will build a rapport with the client. This in turn shows your firm that you are 'a safe pair of hands' who can be trusted with responsibility. The relationship between interviewing and the other skills can be seen in the case study exercises in which you will use the information you obtained in an interview to conduct the rest of the matter. Remember that even if you are not at a stage where you deal with clients on your own, you are still using this skill when your supervisor or another colleague gives you work. The skills you needed to obtain relevant information from a client are equally valid when obtaining information from a colleague.

www.**oxford**interact.com

Introduction

Reflective Learning

Legal Writing

Drafting

Interviewing and Advising

■ **Advocacy**

Practical Legal Research

Section 6

Advocacy

Introduction

Advocacy is the area in which the two branches of the legal profession connect most closely. Advocacy involves many different skills, but the key skill is that of persuasion. In the adversarial system used by the courts in England and Wales, both sides will have the same facts. Disputes may also be about determining the correct version of the facts, where witnesses do not agree, for example. In that case, the court will be making a finding of fact. What each advocate must seek to do is to persuade a judge, a tribunal or a jury that theirs is the correct interpretation or version of those facts.

During your training contract, you can expect to undertake a seat which involves contentious work and this will involve the use of your advocacy skills to some extent. You will also use your advocacy skills in presentations, both to clients and to your colleagues.

The plan below shows the interactive exercises for this skill. It shows the 'path' that you will follow through the exercises, indicated by the arrows that link the exercises. When you go online, remember to sign up to the 'keep me informed' section of the website. This will automatically inform you when new exercises have been added to the site. The blue boxes show the back-up exercises that you will be prompted to undertake before moving on if you score less than 50% of the available marks for the exercise. For example, if you score less than 50% on exercise 4, you will be prompted to complete exercise 4A, to give you a little more practice, before moving on to exercise 5.

The types of exercise vary, although this element includes more video than other interactive elements for fairly obvious reasons! Some of the exercises will focus on preparation and building your case, others will concentrate more on the conduct of hearings including etiquette and forms of question.

In the case study exercises, you will consider the conduct of the tribunal hearing which concludes the case which you will follow from initial interview to its conclusion.

In this section, we will consider a number of aspects of advocacy such as using different types of question to achieve particular results. We will also look at court etiquette, although procedure will not be considered as this is covered in the litigation module of the LPC. We will also be considering some case planning techniques and the important issue of preparation. Finally, we will consider how to learn from your own performances and those of others so that you can develop your skills further.

The SRA's written standards

The standards for advocacy and all other areas of the LPC are available from the SRA website, www.sra.org.uk.

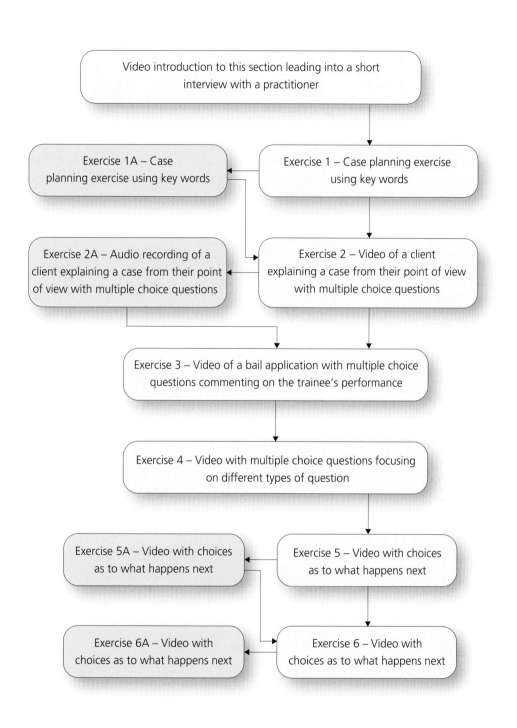

6.1 Dispute resolution

Before considering the skill of advocacy in more detail, it is important to put this skill into context. The court system is often overloaded and litigation is by no means the cheapest or the easiest option. The Solicitors Regulation Authority, the Civil Procedure Rules (CPR) and the legal system generally encourage, and in many cases require, the parties to try and settle their differences without recourse to the courts if possible. While you will consider the options available to your client as part of your civil litigation course, you should always bear them in mind as part of your case preparation process. Failing to consider these options is in breach of Rule 1 of the Code of Conduct, since it cannot be in your client's best interests to always opt for litigation without considering these options first. There may also be penalties under the CPR.

6.2 Advocacy

6.2.1 Preparation

Although it will often be the case that you will not necessarily have interviewed the client or been heavily involved in the preparation of the case, you will always need to be familiar with the subject matter of the case, the key facts, the nature of the application and so on. In many cases, however, your matter will begin with some sort of initial interview with your client. In a criminal matter, for example, you may interview the client at the police station. If you are conducting a civil matter, you will conduct an interview with the client in the same way as for any other type of matter. The detail of interviewing as a skill is covered elsewhere in this book and the associated interactive exercises, but broadly, you should aim to obtain the following from your interview:

- An understanding as to what the matter is about
- A grasp of the key facts (these should be checked with the client during the interview)
- A clear understanding of how you are to proceed. For example, if you are to contact the solicitors for the other side, you should ask for copies of any correspondence so far; this will not only give you a number of points to address, but it will also ensure that you speak to the right person
- Instructions from your client giving you clear guidelines as to their attitude to the matter. For example, if the other side were to offer to settle out of court, what sum would be acceptable
- A list of witnesses (if appropriate) together with their contact details and their involvement in the case. For example, Mrs Jones did not see the car accident, but she saw the defendant punch your client as both drivers got out of their cars

The interactive exercises give you an opportunity to practice case preparation and formulating case theories. For example, exercise 1 asks you to consider the key issues for preparing your case using a short scenario.

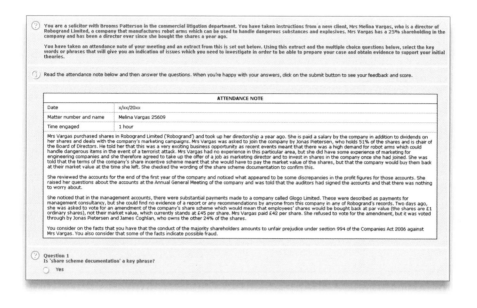

What you require is enough information to build your case – or to make a decision as to whether you actually have a case if there is any doubt. When organizing your information, you may wish to make use of checklists. Checklists are used in many firms' standard procedures in many areas of law, largely because they are a very simple way of ensuring that nothing is forgotten. You may also wish to use diagrams, timelines and simple flowcharts to work out what has happened, how the evidence fits together and how you might wish to proceed.

There are many ways of doing this and you will find a method that suits you, but broadly, all these different planning tools are ways of organizing your facts and your ideas so that you can see how best to proceed. For example, if your matter involves family law or a disputed will, you might wish to draw a family tree.

Example

In the matter of the late Mrs Nwole's intestacy, you are told that the deceased, the widow of the late Olesegun Nwole, had three children, Kayode, Adefemi and Amina. Kayode and Amina predeceased their mother. Adefemi is still alive and has three adult children, Jumoka, Oba and Ekon. Kayode had two sons Aren and Obi. Aren has a daughter, Adeola, who is eight. Obi died two years ago, leaving a daughter, Amadi, who is four. Amina had two children, Sade and Bayo, both of whom are adults.

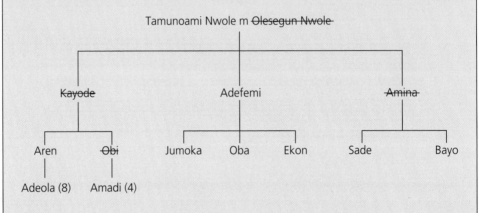

With the family tree, the information is clearer and can be seen at a glance. If you were using this information to determine entitlement on an intestacy, it would be obvious which descendants survived the deceased. It would also be apparent which children would be able to take their parent's share of the estate because they died before the late Tamunoami Nwole.

6.2.2 Timelines

You can also use timelines to plan your case and give you ideas as to how to present the evidence. They may also help you to focus your questions: for example in a criminal matter as you can be precise about times and locations and their relations to each other.

> ### Example
>
> Your client has been accused of armed robbery and you are considering the evidence against him and considering how best to approach the case. You know that your client was at the off-licence at 18:35 and that he left after about 15 minutes as there was a queue. You also know that the security video for the petrol station that your client is accused of robbing shows someone of approximately your client's height arriving at 19:50. The armed robber left at 19:58. Your client's next-door neighbour saw your client coming back from the direction of the off-licence at 20:00.

If you put this information into a timeline, it shows the sequence of events quite clearly:

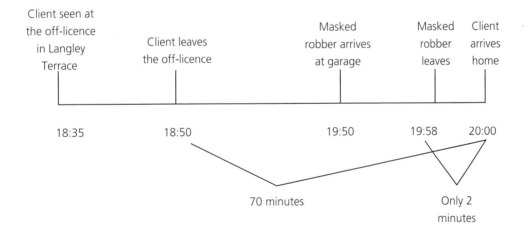

In this timeline, the times at which your client was seen in circumstances in which he could be positively identified – because he was seen by a witness who knows him and because he could be identified on the off-licence security video – would lead you to check the distance between all of these points.

If, for example, the off-licence is close to your client's home, but the scene of the robbery is a 20-minute walk from your client's home, the timeline will cast significant doubt on whether your client could have committed this crime. It would also lead you to check with your client about his movements between leaving the off-licence and to check with the neighbour whether they can be certain that your client walked home; could they have seen if your client was dropped off by car, for example.

A timeline or chronology, where events are listed in a sequence, not necessarily plotted on a line, would also be useful in a civil matter. For example you might use this planning tool in an action for breach of contract, where the timing of consideration passing and the performance of the services required close examination in order to establish whether the contract was enforceable. The chronology would also assist with the presentation of evidence in a logical manner and would help a judge to see the sequence of events should your matter proceed to trial. If it shows weaknesses in the other side's case, it might also be used to settle out of court.

This approach could also help to organize more complex facts, particularly where you will be taking statements from a number of witnesses, some of whose statements may well overlap in terms of the events to which they are testifying. For example, in a sex discrimination case, you may have a number of separate incidents which support your client's case. Some witnesses may be able to attest to a number of incidents. You may wish to use their evidence to give an overview, which can then be supported by the testimony of others to give it additional weight.

6.2.3 Planning

When preparing your case, you will need to plan how to proceed. For example, you will need to consider who is involved and what action you need to take to move your matter forward. There will be time limits, whether self-imposed, set by your client or required by the rules applicable to your matter. Using a chronology and a checklist may be helpful in this case, but a well-organized diary system and reminders (such as an electronic diary system; many firms will use either a well-known software package or a bespoke system) will be invaluable. If you use this type of system, make sure that you input all dates as soon as you can. Give yourself time to actually carry out the necessary work to meet a time limit. Reminding yourself to draft something long and complex on the day it must be submitted will not necessarily be helpful. Exercise 2 gives some practice in case planning and considering how to approach a matter, evidence and so on.

You are a trainee solicitor with Brewbaker Berkeley. You are being supervised by Ellie Freedman, a property lawyer. She asks you to see a client on her behalf and to prepare a case plan for the matter. The client is Mrs Natalia Rubienski, who owns a house in the nearby village of Micklehampstead. She is in dispute with her neighbour who is carrying out building work on the adjoining property. She claims that this has damaged and devalued her property.

Watch the video below and answer the multiple choice questions to build up a case plan and formulate your case theory: the arguments you will use to put your client's case and how those arguments should be presented.

A transcript of this film is available here

Question 1
Mrs Rubienski talks about the environmental and noise pollution as well as the disruption caused by the building work. What role would a discussion on this issue play in your case?

○ The pollution and disruption caused by the building work would be central to your client's case.

○ It is worth referring to the pollution and disruption in your case, but these are not central issues and should not be over-emphasized.

In many firms, you will have a case management system which will usually generate automatic reminders and provide you with a list of deadlines and tasks, some of which the system itself can generate using the information that you input at the start of the matter if it is a routine one – for example bankruptcy or debt recovery proceedings on behalf of a client.

You will also need to ensure that you obtain witness statements and affidavits or sworn statements from those relevant to the matter and file these as required. Evidence from witnesses will provide you with a useful source of detail to add to what you already know and help you to develop a strategy in relation to the case. For example, key facts may emerge from their statements or you may decide that their evidence is not as helpful as you had first thought.

Essential Principles

Remember that while you will want to focus on facts and evidence which support your client's case, you should keep an open mind about your case theory and not simply disregard something just because it does not fit your theory.

6.2.4 Ethics

Once you are admitted to the Roll as a solicitor, your full title is Solicitor of the Supreme Court. This is more than a courtesy or a ceremonial title. The title means that your overriding duty is to the court. The Code of Conduct imposes a requirement to act in the best interests of your client, but this is overridden by your duty to the court where there is a conflict between the two.

This means that you must not lie to the court and you must not knowingly allow your client to do so either. Further, you may not mislead the court, by suppressing, distorting or withholding evidence. Misleading the court is very serious and could lead to you being struck off. This involves having your name removed from the Roll of Solicitors so that you are no longer entitled to practice. You also risk being in contempt of court or possibly a charge of perjury.

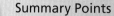

Summary Points

- Preparation is vital to providing your client with a good service and to performing well in your training contract

- Use diagrams and timelines where appropriate

- If your firm uses checklists, make sure you use them. If they don't, consider making your own.

- If your firm uses a case management system, make sure that you understand how it works and what information you need to put in. Ask if you are not sure

- Case theories are not effective if you only consider information which supports them. Be logical and consider all information so that your case theory stands up to scrutiny.

- You owe a duty to the court as well as to your client. Your firm will not be impressed if you do not take professional ethics seriously

6.3 Speaking in public

One aspect of the skill of advocacy is that you need to become used to the sound of your own voice. If you are not used to speaking in public, you will need to consider how you will overcome this. For example, speaking in debates or mooting both provide an excellent opportunity to practise this skill. If you find that the whole experience makes you nervous, you need to devise a method for dealing with your nerves. Obviously you will need to develop your own strategy, but some suggestions are set out below:

- Exercise releases endorphins – 'happy chemicals' which can give you a sense of well-being. You may wish to ensure that you take a break from your preparation to do something active, even for a short while, which can often help to clear your mind and help you to feel calmer and more in control

- Breathing techniques work for some people – deep breathing and relaxation. Again, regimes such as Pilates and yoga emphasize these techniques and instructors can advise on exercises you might want to practise before speaking in public

- Visualization techniques – focus on seeing yourself speaking in court, calm and in control. This is something that will only work if you really want it to. If you find the idea odd and would feel very self-conscious about doing this, it is unlikely to be helpful

How you deal with nerves is very personal, but for public speaking, the most effective way to deal with nerves is to prepare thoroughly and practise as much as you can. Once you have survived public speaking on one occasion, the next becomes less threatening.

 Essential Principles

To help ensure that you can be readily understood, you may wish to slow down slightly from normal conversational speed. This is not to say that you should speak very very slowly so that you sound really patronizing, but nor should you speak so quickly that no one can understand you.

6.3.1 Volume, tone and pitch

These may sound more like issues for a singer than an advocate, but they are important in advocacy and can make a big difference to how you are perceived. If you speak quietly and indistinctly so that the court cannot hear you, the subject matter of your speech, however good, will be lost and you are likely to irritate those listening to you. If, on the other hand, you shout, you will risk coming across as aggressive and rude. You need to ensure that you are audible throughout the court, but not so loud that you sound confrontational. Clear diction is important, but this does not mean that you should aim to sound like a 1950s newsreader! The most important thing is that your listeners can understand what you are saying.

The tone and pitch of what you say will also contribute to the impression that you create. You are aiming to get across to your listeners that you are competent, familiar with your case and a credible advocate. If the tone and pitch of what you say detract from the subject matter, then you need to reconsider your approach. For example, if you allow your nerves to make you speak in a high-pitched squeak, no one will be able to take you seriously.

These points and others are considered in exercise 3, which shows an advocate making a bail application and asks you to comment on the performance.

00:11 01:04

6.3.2 Gestures, eye contact and mannerisms

A well-placed gesture can help to reinforce your point. Gestures used too often or inappropriately will detract from your point and distract your listener.

Eye contact is something that you may not think about when addressing the court. If you try to look your listeners in the eye (although try to avoid aggressively staring them out) when you are speaking, you will naturally hold your head up and your speech will be clearer. If you have notes (which you are likely to do in most advocacy situations), you will need to consider how to make them into a format that enables you to glance at them periodically, rather than keeping your head down because you need to read from them – see later in this section.

Mannerisms can also be very distracting. Fiddling with your hair, spinning your pen or excessive gesticulation can all distract the court from what you are actually saying. An excellent way of determining whether you are detracting from your own speeches is to watch yourself on video or listen to yourself on tape, although video will give you the best indication as to whether your mannerisms and gestures are a distraction. Most LPC providers will video you as part of your advocacy course and you may be given the opportunity to record yourself using a static camera if you need extra practice. Make use of your videos and any feedback that you receive on your performances. You should also assess your own performance honestly and consider what you can learn from it.

Essential Principles

You may wish to ask yourself some or all of the questions below:

- Was my speech clear and easy to understand?

- Did I use gestures sparingly and effectively to make my points?

- Was the pitch and tone of my voice appropriate?

- Did I use repeated distracting mannerisms?

- Did I speak at a pace that made it easy for my listeners to understand me?

- Did I order my speech logically so that my points followed on from each other?

- Was my meaning clear?

- Did I use eye contact appropriately?

- What could I do to improve my performance?

6.4 Persuasion

As we have already considered, a significant part of the skill of advocacy depends on persuasion: giving the person who will be making a decision in your case reasons for accepting your interpretation or version of the facts rather than someone else's.

Ethical considerations and your duty to the court mean that you may not suppress evidence or mislead the court in any way and of course you would not wish to do so. What you must do instead is to consider how you might interpret the same facts differently, or put different facts together in a way that casts a different light on the matter. In doing this, those you seek to persuade must still be convinced that you are genuinely casting doubt on the other side's interpretation. If they consider that you are being disingenuous, the technique may backfire and they will be all the more convinced that the other side is right.

Example

In the 1980s, the Metropolitan Police ran an advertising campaign which showed one man chasing another. Both men were in jeans and jackets. The poster asked the viewer to judge what was happening – was the man who was being pursued being harassed or was he a criminal? In fact, the answer was neither of these things as both men were police officers in plain clothes chasing a third suspect just out of the picture.

What the example shows is that putting information together or looking at it from a different standpoint can persuade those you are addressing to view the evidence differently. This is in no way misleading the court, it is perfectly legitimate.

Example

Witness: 'I heard Mrs Jones say "You can't do that." I then heard a loud crash and the sound of glass smashing followed by Mrs Jones screaming and Mr Jones shouting "What have I done?" I then saw the ambulance arriving to take Mrs Jones to hospital. I saw Mr Jones covered in blood coming out of the house with the ambulance crew.'

Your client, Mr Jones, contends that what Mrs Jones said was part of a conversation they were having about whether he should take the next day off to watch a football match even though he was very busy at work. Mrs Jones then got up to carry a tray of glasses into the house from the garden where they were sitting and tripped over his foot. She fell onto the tray of glasses which smashed and a shard of glass pierced her neck, causing her to bleed heavily. He shouted 'What have I done?' and then tried to staunch the blood. A friend who had been in the house when this happened called the ambulance, but saw nothing of the accident.

You might persuade the court that Mr Jones is telling the truth by asking the witness a number of questions about what she heard and saw. For example:

- You could ask how Mrs Jones sounded when she said 'You can't do that'. If she was being attacked, she would be shouting and might sound hysterical. If it was, as your client contends, part of a conversation, she would sound calm or possibly jocular

- You might ask if she heard anything before this incident. If the neighbour had been in the garden all afternoon and had only heard general conversation, this casts further doubt on the prosecution's suggestion that Mr Jones attacked his wife

- You could also ask if the neighbour had overheard any other arguments or has any reason to believe that there had been previous incidents of domestic violence. If she has not heard anything before, this casts further doubt on the prosecution's interpretation of events

If the witness's answers do cast doubt on the prosecution's case, remind them of this during the closing speech, particularly if the trial is a long one and there has been a lot of evidence.

Remember that persuasion is not just about court appearances. Persuasion is about presenting an argument in a manner which the person you seek to persuade finds compelling. Clarity and simplicity are useful in persuading someone of your point of view. If what you say is clear, easy to understand and makes sense, it is more likely to be acceptable to your listeners and they are more likely to be persuaded that your interpretation is correct.

Resist the temptation to overload them with information so that they have to sift through vast numbers of facts to determine what it is that you are trying to say. Decide which points you want to emphasize and how they link together. If what you are saying is logical in its order and the way that you link facts and ideas together flows well, those you wish to persuade will be able to follow your argument more easily and will at least understand what it is they are being asked to consider. They can then make a judgement about whether they find what you have said sufficiently compelling to change their opinion or to accept your viewpoint if they did not previously have a view on the issue.

In a debate or moot, you might, for example, prepare your argument using what you know to be their key points.

- How might you challenge them?
- Can you refute or cast doubt on their application to the matter?
- Can you point out any weaknesses in their chain of reasoning which might cause them to reconsider their view?
- Are there additional facts which they do not take into account that might persuade them that they may need to rethink?

The points made earlier about pitch, tone, gestures etc will all add weight to what you are saying. If your audience consider that you are credible as an advocate, they will be more likely to take what you say seriously and be persuaded by it.

> **Summary Points**
>
> - Practise speaking in public if you can – making a contribution in your LPC sessions also counts!
> - If you can watch yourself on video, do so. Seeing how you perform when speaking can be incredibly helpful and will give you a chance to reflect and improve
> - Think about how you sound to others and use the checklist to consider what you could do to improve
> - Ask your tutor for help and guidance if you are finding this (or any other skill) difficult
> - Remember that you are seeking to persuade. If what you say is well prepared, logically ordered and clear, you will be a lot more effective
> - Keep it simple, but don't be patronizing
> - Use gestures sparingly – don't let them be a distraction

6.5 Different types of hearing

During your training contract, you will not have the right to appear in open court. You will have the right to appear in some types of hearing in the Magistrates' Court, the County Court and some tribunals. In the High Court, you may appear in chambers (hearings which are not in open court).

Even once you are qualified, your rights of audience will be limited unless and until you take a further qualification which will give you higher rights of audience: the right to appear in the higher courts in civil and criminal matters.

If you have the opportunity to do so, try to sit in on court hearings during your LPC. Some hearings are open to the public and it can be a useful opportunity to observe experienced advocates in action and pick up a few tips. It can also give you an idea of court etiquette, forms of address and so on.

Not all hearings will be trials. There may be interim applications to the court, applications for costs and so on. You may find your first few court appearances very brief and indeed in most cases the court now conducts interim hearings by telephone conference to save time and court resources.

6.5.1 Etiquette

Whichever type of hearing you are conducting, you will need to be familiar with the correct etiquette for that particular court. Some points of etiquette will apply to you even if you are not actually speaking. For example, you should stand up when asked to do so and observe silence when others are speaking. In some courts you do not have to stand up to speak. In courts where you are required to stand up to speak, if your opponent stands up, you should sit down, even if they are interrupting you. If you wish to speak while the other side is doing so, you should stand before speaking, not simply interrupt.

Each court or forum will have a form of address which is appropriate to use when addressing those presiding and other participants in the process. The table below gives some examples.

Forum	Who hears your case or application?	Form of address
Tribunal	A panel	Sir, Madam
Magistrates' Court	Magistrates (a bench if more than one)	Sir, Madam
County Court	A District judge	Sir, Madam
High Court	A High Court judge	My Lord, My Lady or Your Lordship, Your Ladyship

In addition, you would usually refer to counsel as 'my learned friend' (pronounced 'my learnéd friend') and to another solicitor in court as 'my friend'.

Failure to observe correct etiquette will have a variety of consequences depending on what breach you commit. The most serious of these is contempt of court, which can result in a custodial sentence. At best, you will make yourself look foolish and, if your blunder is reported back to your firm, you will not exactly impress your supervisor. In particular, unless you are carrying a hearing involving children or vulnerable witnesses, forms of language and address are usually impersonal. You would not, for example, refer to your client, or indeed anyone else, by their first name.

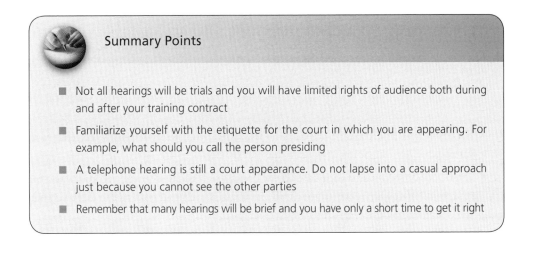

Summary Points

- Not all hearings will be trials and you will have limited rights of audience both during and after your training contract
- Familiarize yourself with the etiquette for the court in which you are appearing. For example, what should you call the person presiding
- A telephone hearing is still a court appearance. Do not lapse into a casual approach just because you cannot see the other parties
- Remember that many hearings will be brief and you have only a short time to get it right

6.5.2 Bail applications

Before moving on to consider the main types of speech in a trial, it is helpful to consider bail applications as these will be needed before the trial as part of the preliminary hearings. There is a right to bail in most circumstances and it is the prosecution's task to persuade the court that the client will, for example:

- Fail to surrender to custody; or
- Commit an offence while on bail; or
- Interfere with witnesses or otherwise obstruct the course of justice, whether in relation to himself or any other person

There are a number of factors that the court will take into account when determining bail, but broadly, they will weigh up the risks and decide accordingly. For example, if your client has a family, a mortgage and a job, these will make it less likely that they will abscond. The above list is not exhaustive.

This is obviously a very brief summary of a complex area which will be addressed in your litigation module. The entire area has been reviewed by the Law Commission in the light of the Human Rights Act 1998. In addition, the right to bail is not as clear-cut as it might sound, with the Bail Act 1976 provisions now subject to the Criminal Justice Act 1994.

In making your application, you should consider the facts of your client's case in the light of the legislation, case law and practice in this area. You will then need to use any factors which will refute or cast doubt on the points raised by the prosecution in their submissions as to why bail should be refused. You could either refer to each point individually, addressing the concerns of the other side on each issue, or, if there is more than one issue which can be addressed by a particular fact or legal point, group your points together. This may be less repetitious for the court and will save time at the hearing.

6.5.3 Opening speeches in court and tribunals

In most civil cases, opening speeches are no longer standard practice. However, if your matter does require an opening speech, whichever side you are for in your hearing, this should serve a number of purposes. Your speech should:

- Establish you as a credible advocate – those listening to you should feel that you know what you are doing and that they can trust you
- Introduce both you and your case to the court – tell them who you are and who you represent (in some courts, you will fill out a slip which you pass to the clerk so that the court knows who you are)

- Introduce your case to those judging it. Say briefly what you intend to establish and give a short summary of how you intend to do this. What you say here should come as no surprise to the other side who should already have your evidence

Everything that was considered earlier with regard to clarity, volume and so on should be applied to your speech.

Most advocates will make notes for their speeches beforehand. This can be very useful in terms of ensuring that nothing is forgotten, but be careful that you do not simply read your notes aloud.

Reading from what is effectively a script is not regarded as good practice. If you do this, your delivery is likely to be stilted and wooden. You are also more likely to be indistinct and difficult to understand as you will have to either hold the paper up in front of you or look down as you read. It will also be difficult to keep eye contact with your listeners. If you do use notes, which is generally a sound idea, you should consider some alternatives to simply writing out a script.

Essential Principles

Note cards are often used to condense a speech to its key points. They are designed to prompt you, not to be read out like a script. If you use a number of cards, you may wish to hold them together in order using a treasury tag through the corner of each card. This will allow you to keep them in order, but flip through them quickly as you make your points.

Mind maps are also worth considering as a way of making notes. They are considered in more detail in the interviewing section of this book. Mind maps allow you to make your points in a visual format, with each point linked to connected points and followed through to its conclusion.

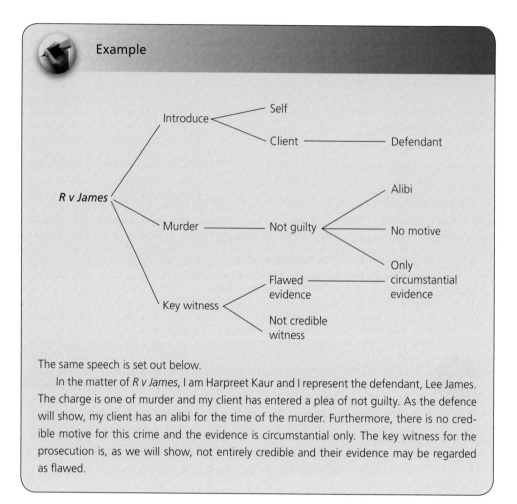

Example

The same speech is set out below.

In the matter of *R v James*, I am Harpreet Kaur and I represent the defendant, Lee James. The charge is one of murder and my client has entered a plea of not guilty. As the defence will show, my client has an alibi for the time of the murder. Furthermore, there is no credible motive for this crime and the evidence is circumstantial only. The key witness for the prosecution is, as we will show, not entirely credible and their evidence may be regarded as flawed.

If you were making this speech using your notes, you might find the visual representation easier to follow if you were trying to ensure that your delivery was clear and that you maintained eye contact with the members of the jury and other listeners.

6.5.4 Questions

During the course of your matter, you will have to consider the evidence and question any witnesses. This is covered in much more detail in your professional skills course, but an understanding of questioning techniques is generally helpful. There are two types of 'examination' of a witness. The examination in chief is the process of questioning by the party who has called the witness. In civil matters, examination in chief is not generally used now, as the witnesses' evidence is contained in their statements. In a criminal matter, if a witness has been called by the prosecution, the prosecution advocate will conduct the examination in chief. The other side (the defence in this case) will conduct a cross-examination. The examination in chief is designed to draw out the witness's story. In order to do this, the advocate will use two main types of question.

Open questions are questions to which a 'yes' or 'no' answer would be in inappropriate. Equally, short or one or two word answers would not normally be given to this type of question. Generic examples include

- 'Why?'
- 'When?'
- 'Describe'
- 'What?'
- 'How?'
- 'Explain'

The object of a question of this type is to draw out the witness's story as much as possible. This type of question invites the person answering to be expansive: to tell their story. Be careful when asking this type of question during the examination in chief that the question is not 'leading'. Leading questions during the examination in chief are not permitted. A leading question is one which effectively invites the person being questioned to give a particular answer, leading them in the direction of your choice, rather than allowing them to answer openly.

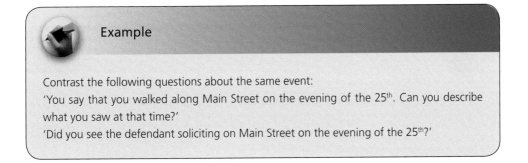

Example

Contrast the following questions about the same event:
'You say that you walked along Main Street on the evening of the 25th. Can you describe what you saw at that time?'
'Did you see the defendant soliciting on Main Street on the evening of the 25th?'

The first question asks the witness to describe the facts. The second leads them as to what they should be saying – suggesting that the defendant was soliciting, rather than leaving the witness to tell their story and allowing the evidence to emerge.

The other main type of question is the closed question. Closed questions are those which require a 'yes' or 'no' answer or a brief statement of fact.

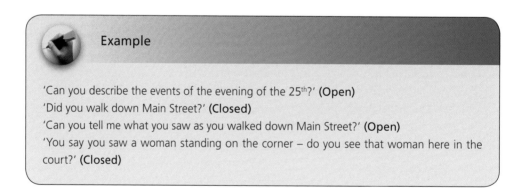

> **Example**
>
> 'Can you describe the events of the evening of the 25th?'
> 'Were you on Main Street at 11:30 on the 25th?'

The first version invites the witness to tell their story. The second invites a 'yes' or 'no' answer.

This is not to suggest that open questions are good and closed questions are bad. Both are very useful, but are used for different purposes. If you want a witness to confirm a particular fact or a number of facts and nothing more, a closed question will serve this purpose. Often, when questioning a witness, a mixture of open and closed questions will be used.

The type of question is varied so that the witness will be able to tell their story, but in a controlled way which does not waste the court's time and will give emphasis to the points most relevant to your case. A closed question asked during the course of a witness's answer to an open question can add emphasis to a key point.

> **Example**
>
> 'Can you describe the events of the evening of the 25th?' **(Open)**
> 'Did you walk down Main Street?' **(Closed)**
> 'Can you tell me what you saw as you walked down Main Street?' **(Open)**
> 'You say you saw a woman standing on the corner – do you see that woman here in the court?' **(Closed)**

During your examination in chief, the witness should not be saying anything that you do not expect. Your witness will have given a witness statement as part of your case preparation and there should be no surprises. In the event that the witness does not 'come up to proof' – they depart from their statement – you may wish to use closed questions to bring them back on track, but without using leading questions. If you cannot do this, you may have to apply to the court to treat the witness as hostile. In this case, the witness does not appear to be answering your questions in a way which is consistent with their witness statement. If the court allows you to treat them as hostile, you may cross-examine your own witness and confront them with their previous statement, requiring them to explain the inconsistencies which led you to treat them as hostile.

6.5.5 The other side's speeches and examinations

When your opponent is speaking, resist the temptation to take a break and switch off until it is your turn to speak again. Listening is an important part of advocacy as well because it enables you to respond to points raised by the other side or to spot and exploit weaknesses in their arguments. When you are at any type of hearing, thinking on your feet and taking any opportunities presented to you by the other side can make a big difference.

You could note down any key points that arise and make use of them in your closing speech, or use them to cross-examine the other side's witness later on in the matter. For example, they might contradict themselves on a point, or depart from their statement in a small way, which would allow you to cast doubt on their evidence later.

6.5.6 Cross-examination

The purpose of cross-examination is to exploit weaknesses in the witness's testimony. Leading questions are permitted when cross-examining as the testimony has already been given. Contrast this with the position during the examination in chief, where a leading question could give rise to an objection on the part of the advocate for the other side.

Closed questions would be fairly common here although an open question on a weak point which leads the witness to flounder and contradict themselves would help your client's case.

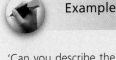 **Example**

'Can you describe the conditions as you walked down Main Street on the evening of the 25th?' **(Open)**

'Were all the street lights on Main Street working?' **(Closed)**

'Describe where the defendant was standing on Main Street in relation to the street lights.' **(Open)**

'You say that you saw the defendant on the corner of Main Street. You have just told us that the street light closest to the defendant was broken and that it was dark. Given what you have just told us, can you be entirely certain that it was the defendant that you saw?' **(Closed)**

In all situations where you are questioning a witness, be careful that you do not use a number of closed questions one after the other. This style can be perceived as aggressive and should be used sparingly, particularly if you are concerned that you may alienate a jury or judge. Equally, too many open questions may mean that the witness loses focus and their evidence does not hold the attention of the court. A careful mix of questions is usually the most effective approach.

In exercises 5 and 6, you are asked to select what should happen next, including what type of question should be asked at a number of different points. This is designed to give you some practice in deciding what type of question would be appropriate in a variety of situations.

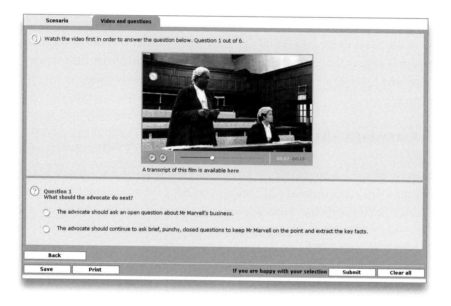

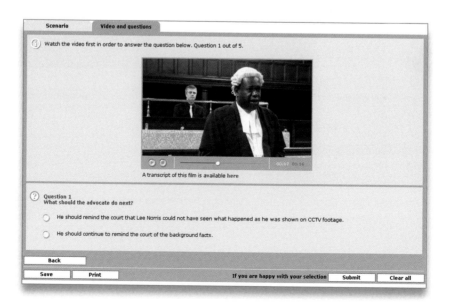

Additionally, exercise 5 in the case study gives you the opportunity to choose what should happen next during a cross-examination.

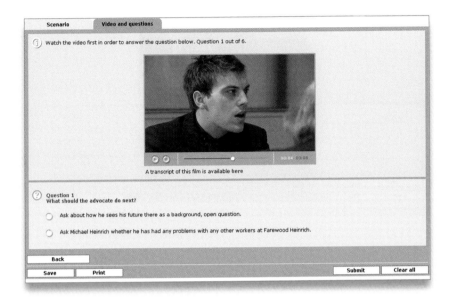

6.5.7 Closing speeches

Closing speeches are designed to pull together the threads of what has gone before and remind the court or tribunal of the key points in your case. During the course of the case, you should note anything relevant which has emerged during the case that you can draw on to support the conclusion you wish to achieve.

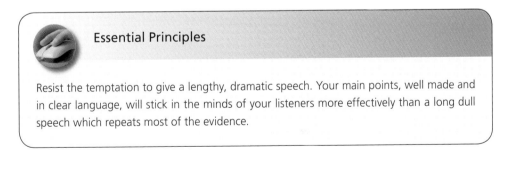

Essential Principles

Resist the temptation to give a lengthy, dramatic speech. Your main points, well made and in clear language, will stick in the minds of your listeners more effectively than a long dull speech which repeats most of the evidence.

Again, you are likely to need notes to use in your closing speech – see earlier in this section. Exercise 6 gives you the opportunity to view a closing speech and asks questions on its effectiveness.

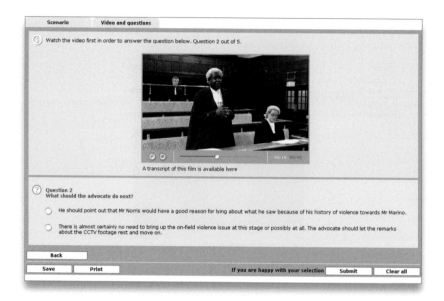

6.5.8 Pleas in mitigation

If your client is found guilty of a criminal offence, you will need to make a plea in mitigation which may be taken into account when sentencing your client. Effectively, you are persuading the court that your client should not receive the harshest penalty, but should be treated more leniently. This is a complex area and this paragraph is intended to provide only a brief introduction. The details as to procedure and the factors that the court would take into account are part of criminal litigation.

For example, where an offence carries either a custodial sentence or a non-custodial penalty, you would want to present to the court reasons why it would be better for a non-custodial penalty to be imposed. If your client is the only doctor in a small, isolated village, imposing a custodial sentence for a driving offence which did not result in a fatality would be to the detriment of the community and a sentence of community service might be a more effective alternative.

If you were acting for a parent convicted of shoplifting who has no previous convictions, you would refer to the fact that they have young children who might have to go into local authority care if a custodial sentence were to be imposed.

As with any other advocacy, the issues of clarity and so on apply, as do those of avoiding the temptation to be dramatic and long-winded.

6.5.9 Costs in civil matters

The court will determine who is to pay costs in a civil matter at a number of points during the conduct of the matter. For example, if there are interim hearings, the court will consider who is to bear the costs of these, as well as who will pay the costs overall. It will not always be the losing party who pays the costs. The court may rule that each side should bear their own costs if they consider that this would be just. It is also possible that the winning party might have the costs awarded against them if the court feels that although they have won technically, they have perhaps acted in a way which the court feels is unfair.

When making an application for costs, you should consider any factors which you think are appropriate to put before the court in persuading them that your client should not bear the costs. These might include:

- Delays by the other side which have increased your costs or wasted the court's time
- Unconscionable behaviour by the other side, particularly if they have been criticized for this by the court
- If your client won the case, you might cite the reasons given in the judgment which would support your claim
- If your opponent is a large corporate entity and your client is an individual, it may be worth reminding the court of this fact, although it may backfire if your client brought the action and has been criticized by the court for doing so

Overall, what you are seeking to do is to ensure that the court is reminded of any relevant factors that would divert them from an intention to award costs against your client.

6.6 Following up the hearing

This is included for the sake of completeness. In your LPC, you would cover this issue in your litigation module, although it is helpful to consider it briefly in context at this point. In many cases, the court will draw up any order that it makes, although in some cases you may have agreed an order before the hearing which both sides are asking the court to ratify. If the court draws up the order, you will receive a copy which you should then check carefully. Most judges and magistrates will have a computer in the court which they can use to draw up the order at the time of the hearing if it is straightforward.

Other follow-up actions will be determined by the nature of the case and your firm's procedures, but they will include billing and may include dealing with the assessment of costs if appropriate, arranging for the enforcement of an order, writing to your client to explain the order, preparing an appeal and so on.

As a point of professional conduct, you should have discussed costs with your client initially, including the risk that they might have to pay the other side's costs as well as yours. You also have an obligation to keep your client informed about costs as the matter progresses. There should therefore be no surprises for your client, but you may still have to handle the issue of costs with some tact, especially if they have not achieved the outcome that they wanted.

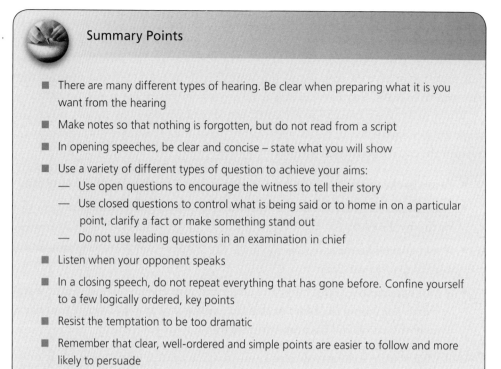

Summary Points

- There are many different types of hearing. Be clear when preparing what it is you want from the hearing
- Make notes so that nothing is forgotten, but do not read from a script
- In opening speeches, be clear and concise – state what you will show
- Use a variety of different types of question to achieve your aims:
  - Use open questions to encourage the witness to tell their story
  - Use closed questions to control what is being said or to home in on a particular point, clarify a fact or make something stand out
  - Do not use leading questions in an examination in chief
- Listen when your opponent speaks
- In a closing speech, do not repeat everything that has gone before. Confine yourself to a few logically ordered, key points
- Resist the temptation to be too dramatic
- Remember that clear, well-ordered and simple points are easier to follow and more likely to persuade

6.7 Conclusion

Advocacy is a key skill which you will need to master for the purpose of your assessment, your training contract and, if you decide to pursue a career in litigation, in your future career.

Learning to speak in public with confidence is part of this skill and one that you can develop to a great extent by watching any videos of yourself and assessing the effectiveness of your performance. Preparation is also a key component in your successful performance. However, you should also bear in mind that while preparation takes you a long way, paying close attention to what others are saying and taking advantage of any opportunities this gives you will also stand you in good stead. You will need to think on your feet and listen, as opposed to waiting until it is your turn to speak again. If you can do these things, you are well on the way to mastering the skill and becoming an effective advocate.

www.**oxford**interact.com

Introduction

Reflective Learning

Legal Writing

Drafting

Interviewing and Advising

Advocacy

■ **Practical Legal Research**

Section 7

Practical Legal Research

Introduction

This section and the interactive exercises which it accompanies consider the skill of practical legal research. The section takes you through the key issues, but is slightly different to the other modules in that some of the exercises are available to print out before completion. There is more detail on these exercises in the explanatory paragraph that you will find at the end of this section.

In many ways, the name of the skill says it all:

Essential Principles

- It has to be practical; resist the temptation to write an essay on the points of academic interest

- It concerns law (although the practical and commercial aspects of the matter will influence the advice that you give)

- It is research. You are being asked to carry out this work because the person who asked you to do so does not know the answer and wants you to find it

- In addition, it has to be up to date. Always check for updates and say that you did, even if there are no changes as a result

During your training contract, you will frequently be asked to carry out research. It may seem an obvious point, but remember that the solicitor asking you to do this does not have a model answer. They are asking you to carry out the research because they want to know the answer and are expecting you to use your skills to find it. They will also expect you to provide them with a record of research that they can follow easily and conclusions that are expressed briefly and coherently. If you can do this task well, you should have frequent opportunities to shine. If you do it poorly, it can only undermine your efforts to be seen as the kind of trainee that a firm will want to keep on at the end of your contract.

In the short term, you will have Practical Legal Research assessments during your LPC. If you have difficulties with this area, you will need to address them at an early stage. The exercises available to print out, together with those in the interactive resource should give you plenty of practice, but as with any skill, if you are in difficulties, you should speak to a tutor.

The exercises for this module are set out in the 'map' below. The arrows between the exercises show the path you will follow, including, in some cases, the supplementary exercises which you will be prompted to complete in the event that you score less than 50% of the available marks in an initial exercise.

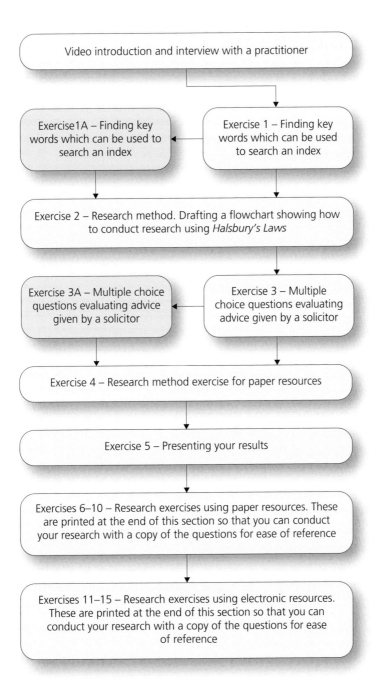

The exercises in the blue boxes are supplementary exercises which you will be prompted to complete before moving on if you score less than 50% in the initial exercise. It is also possible to complete these exercises even if you scored more than 50% if you feel you would like more practice.

7.1 **No essays, please**

When approaching Practical Legal Research as a skill, the first thing you need to accept is that you are not writing an essay. Your academic career to date is likely to have been based around writing essays. You now need to understand that this is something different and deal with it accordingly. Your assessor and your firm will be unimpressed by lengthy academic digressions, however interesting and well written they may be.

Part of the difference between what you have done previously and what you are doing now is the length of what is required. In an academic essay, you would normally expect to work to a guideline about the number of words you should produce. This is not the case with legal research.

If your findings and recommendations seem brief, ask yourself whether you have included everything that your reader needs to advise the client and follow your research. If they have, resist the temptation to 'pad' your memo or record. No trainee solicitor ever had a memo returned to them because it was less than 3,000 words. They have frequently had memos returned because they did not contain relevant information, or because the research path was incomplete or difficult to follow.

7.2 **Some practical points**

Remember that in practice, the client is paying the costs of the matter. On the LPC, you will have many other calls on your time. In both cases, try not to spend too much time on your research, but balance this with the need to be thorough. A piece of research which overlooks something important because it was rushed is not acceptable, but neither is a piece of research which took many hours for which a client is not prepared to pay or which prevented you from carrying out other tasks.

When you are conducting research, it is helpful to make notes of what you find (and where you found it) as you go. This enables you and your reader to retrace your steps if necessary. It is also helpful to put in enough information to allow someone to follow your research, but not so much that it becomes confusing.

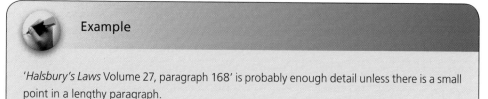

Example

'*Halsbury's Laws* Volume 27, paragraph 168' is probably enough detail unless there is a small point in a lengthy paragraph.

'*Halsbury's Laws* Volume 27, paragraph 168, lines 12, 13, 14, 15, 16 and 20' is possibly going too far unless you are selecting different parts of the paragraph and weeding out irrelevance.

There is a temptation to cut and paste text from online sources, for example, sections from a statute. This should always be approached with caution. It is helpful to include extracts from statutory or case material, but only to the extent that you need to do so and never without some commentary. Cutting and pasting large amounts of such material without comment is never a good idea, not least because your reader is busy and will not want to wade through large volumes of text, much of which may be irrelevant, in order to find what they need.

If you do quote from statute or anything else for that matter, it is essential that you make it clear that you are quoting as failing to do this is plagiarism. Using quotation marks or italics are accepted ways of doing this. You should also cite any sources that you use. For example, state the Act and section, the case and its reference or the text, author and edition.

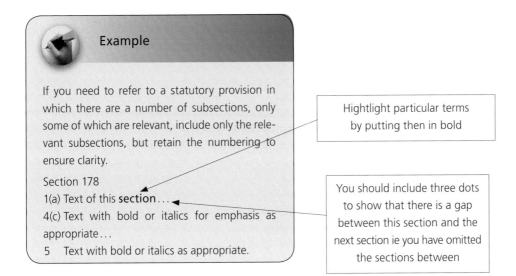

Example

If you need to refer to a statutory provision in which there are a number of subsections, only some of which are relevant, include only the relevant subsections, but retain the numbering to ensure clarity.

Section 178
1(a) Text of this **section** . . .
4(c) Text with bold or italics for emphasis as appropriate . . .
5   Text with bold or italics as appropriate.

Hightlight particular terms by putting then in bold

You should include three dots to show that there is a gap between this section and the next section ie you have omitted the sections between

If all the intervening sections (which are not relevant) had been shown, this would have made it difficult for your reader to follow and wasted their time.

Sometimes in your research, you will consider a possible solution or a provision which looks as though it might be productive, but turns out not to be relevant. It is often worth stating that you have considered and rejected such a point. Be brief and explain why you eliminated the point, but always consider whether it is worth mentioning. In some cases, it will save extra work if a query as to whether that point is, in fact, relevant, arises. If it does, you have already addressed the issue.

Be careful not to do this too often if you can avoid it. Showing one or two such 'blind alleys' is likely to be acceptable, giving details of ten is, in most cases, unlikely to be regarded as good practice. Use your judgement to determine whether this information is worth including.

Remember that this is about the client, even if the client is fictitious and forms part of an assessment question. Always bear in mind their aims when carrying out research. This should help you to keep on track and avoid distractions from interesting, but not necessarily relevant points.

On a similar point, you need to come to a conclusion, but do not be too peremptory when suggesting that a course of action is taken. A senior partner is unlikely to take kindly to being ordered to do something by a trainee!

Summary Points

- No essays: accept that this is a different kind of writing
- There is no minimum word limit. Be brief, but don't leave out relevant information
- Remember that costs are an issue in practice. Don't spend too much time, but spend enough to produce something thorough
- Make it easy for your reader; remember that they are busy
- Note your research steps as you go; it makes it easier to check and write up
- Put in enough information to allow your reader to follow you, but not so much that they cannot see your point for references
- Don't cut and paste large chunks of undigested text
- Clearly attribute text written by someone else, whether it is statute, case law or commentary, to avoid plagiarism
- This is about the client, so keep their aims in mind
- Points that were eliminated can be useful, but not too many
- Come to a conclusion, but don't issue orders

7.3 Research in a practical context

In practice, you are likely to receive information about issues for research from a number of sources:

- An interview with a client
- Information or a request from a solicitor asking you to conduct some research for a client
- Requests for research on an issue for a briefing (whether you or a solicitor will be giving the briefing)

Your assessments on the LPC are likely to simulate these sources of information, for example by giving you a fact pattern and asking you to advise. Check your provider's assessment guidance for more detail.

Whatever the source of information, you will need to consider exactly what it is that you are being asked to do.

7.3.1 Client's objectives

If a client comes to see you about an employment problem, they may want their job back, or they may want to resolve the dispute with their employer in some other way. They may, for example, wish to sue for constructive dismissal. Do not assume that you know what your client wants; always ask. They may not be aware of the alternatives available to them. It is for you to help them make an informed choice, not to assume that you know what is best.

For example, if the client wanted their job back and you spent time researching constructive dismissal, you would waste time and possibly miss opportunities to resolve the matter. This is not to say that you should never consider options or alternatives (for example if what the client wants is not practical or they have no right to that particular remedy), merely that you need to ensure that you focus your research on areas that are appropriate. This will avoid wasted time and costs incurred which you cannot bill.

7.3.2 Key words

Key words are considered in the context of a number of other skills. They will help you to decide a number of things including:

- The relevant areas of law (remember that there may well be more than one)
- The client's aims and objectives; what is it that they want to achieve?
- Any factors that would affect your advice. For example, what is the client's attitude to risk? Are there commercial, confidentiality or professional conduct issues to take into account?

Key words can also prompt you to take practical steps such as follow-up measures and key dates for future actions.

In some cases, it will be more a question of what your client needs, rather than what they want to achieve. The obvious example is when you are advising a client who is charged with committing a criminal offence. Their objective is to be acquitted, but this may not be achievable in the circumstances.

In most other cases, your client will have an objective or a number of objectives. Part of the skill of practical legal research is determining what the client's objectives actually are and then ensuring that they drive your research, conclusions and advice.

In the interactive resource, there are exercises which require you to select key words from an attendance note to determine the areas for research. For example in exercise 1 you will be asked to select the key words in a scenario for research.

⑦ You are acting for Boleslav Grabowski who has asked you for advice about his business. He owns a bookbinding business which specializes in the restoration of old books. He is considering employing Judith Mirman as a bookbinder. She claims to have extensive experience and has provided references. Mr Grabowski would like to employ Judith, but he wants to know if he can take her on for a probationary period only.

ⓘ Select **two** of the following words or phrases that you would use when checking the index as part of your research into Mr Grabowski's problem.

○ References

○ Employment

○ Probation

○ Probationary employment

○ Bookbinding

○ Employee

○ Restoration

○ Specialist

| Save | Print | | If you are happy with your selection | Submit | Clear all |

Example

There are key words in the following passage which tell you the areas of law and the client's objectives. They also indicate practical steps which should be taken.

The client tells you that they have made an <u>agreement</u> with a business <u>partner</u> which includes provisions relating to the <u>division of profits</u>.

The client goes on to say that a large order was secured after the agreement was signed, but their business partner <u>backdated the order</u> in order to avoid sharing the profits. Your client considers this to be <u>fraudulent</u> and wants to <u>terminate the agreement</u> and <u>sue for damages</u>.

The key words tell you the following:

Areas of law

Agreement – contract law
Partner – partnership law
Backdated the order, fraudulent – criminal law

Client's objectives

Terminate the agreement
Sue for damages

Practical steps

Division of profits – look at the agreement

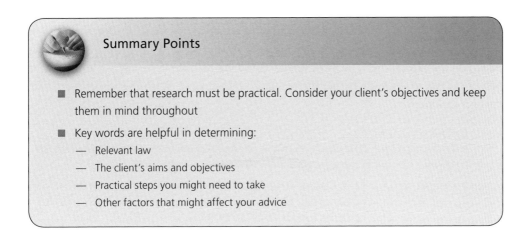

Summary Points

■ Remember that research must be practical. Consider your client's objectives and keep them in mind throughout

■ Key words are helpful in determining:
— Relevant law
— The client's aims and objectives
— Practical steps you might need to take
— Other factors that might affect your advice

7.4 Resources

The resources that you have available to you will vary, depending on your LPC provider and, later, on your firm. Your firm might, for example, make use of your local Law Society Library, rather than having an extensive in-house library, or you might have access to some electronic resources and not others. Do not assume that paper resources are inferior to electronic or vice versa. Both have their place and you should ensure that you can use both effectively. It is not possible to give a comprehensive tour of any and all resources to which you might have access. There are, however, some resources which are present in all law libraries and others which are accessible free of charge using the internet. These will be considered briefly, but you should be aware that web-based resources change frequently and are highly variable in terms of how much you can rely on them.

7.4.1 Electronic resources

The major providers such as Westlaw and LexisNexis Butterworths will often provide in-house training to LPC providers and, in some cases, to firms. If you do not receive 'live' training, the resources provide interactive tutorials and 'Help' functions to ensure that you can use them effectively.

Many law firms will have information on current legal issues on their websites and some will have an email notification service. Many firms and individual lawyers now blog and this can provide you with useful insights into how practising lawyers are approaching current legal points. Obviously these are likely to be fairly subjective, but that does not detract from their usefulness as a place to get an overview or to pick up on a topical issue which may be helpful to one of your matters or to your LPC course. Some firms and publishers provide podcasts for download, often using the iTunes ™ software.

Regulatory bodies and government departments are often useful sources of information but you should be careful when accessing statutory materials in this way. This is because in most cases you will be accessing the statute as it was at Royal Assent. Later amendments will not necessarily be included and you will not have any references in the text of the Act to suggest whether there might have been any. With this caveat, some useful sites include:

http://www.direct.gov.uk/en/index.htm	This site gives links to a range of government sites including sites for crime, justice and the law. This also includes the court service.
http://www.hmrc.gov.uk	This is the main site for taxation. It is an amalgamation of the previous sites for the Inland Revenue and HM Customs & Excise. It includes access to manuals for the taxation authorities, which can provide useful insights into how HMRC are likely to interpret the facts of your client's matter.
http://www.dca.gov.uk/procedurerules.htm	This site provides links to civil and criminal procedure rules and other useful information regarding contentious matters.
http://www.parliament.uk	This site gives details of legislation which is pending, as well as all new legislation since 1988 (1987 for Statutory Instruments). The legislation is in its original form so approach with caution and always check for updates using another source, whether paper or electronic.
http://www.fsa.gov.uk	This is the site for the Financial Services Authority. They are responsible for regulating financial services providers (including solicitors who provide certain services) and for money laundering prevention.
http://www.lawsociety.org.uk/home.law http://www.sra.org.uk	These are the sites for the representative and regulatory organizations which govern solicitors.
http://www.lawbore.net	This is a site which links to a number of useful legal sites for law students.
http://www.venables.co.uk/sites.htm	This is a site with a list of links to useful resources for lawyers including human rights and other free legal services.
http://www.biicl.org	This site covers both British and international law.
http://www.step.org	The Society of Trust and Estate Practitioners provides information on current issues for trust and estate practitioners (who include many lawyers practising in this area).
http://www.tax.org.uk	The Chartered Institute of Tax is a separate professional body of tax practitioners.
http://www.insolvency-practitioners.org.uk	The Insolvency Practitioners Association is a professional body for those specializing in this area.

| http://www.ip-institute.org.uk | The Intellectual Property Institute provides articles and links to other sites for those whose work involves this area of law. |
| http://europa.eu/index_en.htm | A wealth of free information on European legal, tax and other issues. |

Clearly this is not an exhaustive list and new sites will become available all the time. As with any research, ensure that you check any information for updates and use primary sources as authority for any advice wherever possible.

With regard to subscription services, your firm or provider will be able to give you more information about the resources to which they subscribe so that you are aware of what you have at your disposal when carrying out research.

Searching electronic resources

When you search any electronic resource, you need to choose your search terms with care. Each individual resource will have some guidance about searching and you should review any guidelines, tips etc before searching.

There are a number of different ways in which you can search most electronic resources. Remember that you need a balance between something quite vague and something very precise. A vague search term or a very general one may throw out thousands of hits which you then need to review, which is time consuming and frustrating. On the other hand, if you are searching for something very precise, there is a risk that you will miss important points or end up with no hits because there is no exact match.

Most resources will make use of connectors and again, there should be guidance on this point in the resource itself. You will usually be able to search for a specific phrase (if you are very sure of your ground and are looking for a particular point), but you will often have to put this in brackets or quotes in order to search for it as a phrase, rather than looking for each of its component terms individually.

You should also check for guidance as to what connectors to use if you want to search for terms as alternatives (find all the paragraphs or sections in this work which contain either of the two search terms, for example). The other possibility is to find paragraphs or sections which contain both or all of your search terms. This is very useful if one or more of your search terms is very common. All the electronic research exercises in this module require you to consider this issue.

(?) Before attempting this exercise, you need to undertake research on Problem 7 featured on page 151 of your *LPC Skills Online* text book. If you have not done this, click 'Save' and 'Log out' in order to undertake your research. You should ensure that you complete your research using ELECTRONIC resources before attempting to answer the multiple choice questions below. The question from the book which accompanies this resource is reproduced below:

You are acting for Bartomeu Ferrer, who runs a wine importation and mail order business. He has fewer than 25 employees, who are managed by Mark Newsome. Mark recently had an affair with another employee, which caused very bad feeling among the workforce. As a result, business has been disrupted. Mr Ferrer cannot afford to allow this disruption to continue and would like Mr Newsome to leave his employ. He is prepared to make him a generous offer if he leaves, although there is nothing in the contract of employment which allows him to do this. Mr Newsome has indicated that he would be prepared to agree to this as he would like to start his own business and is finding the atmosphere at work almost unbearable. He would not be prepared to resign without any payment as he would not be able to start his own business without any capital. Mr Ferrer has heard that it is possible to make a payment of up to £30,000 tax free to an employee who leaves by agreement. He also wants Mr Newsome to give up his right to sue later for his dismissal and wants him to sign some sort of agreement confirming that he will not take Mr Ferrer to a tribunal. Advise Mr Ferrer.

(i) Research Problem 7 independently of this web site, using the resources available to you in your law library. Next, answer the multiple choice questions below which will help you to determine how effective and thorough your research has been. When you're happy with your answers, click on the 'Submit' button to see your score and feedback. A suggested answer is available to print off at the end of this exercise.

(?) **Question 1**
What is the client trying to achieve?

○ The client wishes to dismiss an employee without giving rise to a claim against him, either now or in future. He wants to know if this can be done in a tax-efficient manner.

○ The client wishes to dismiss an employee who is disrupting his business in a tax-efficient manner.

○ The client wishes to pay a capital sum to an employee to ensure that no claim is made against him.

(?) **Question 2**
Which terms did you use for your search?

○ Employee, resign, lump sum.

○ Employee, tax.

○ Dismissal, employee, tax.

Example

If you are researching an exercise which requires you to consider an issue of dismissal in connection with the transfer of a business undertaking, you could enter a number of possible different terms:

Employment	This will result in a huge number of hits and the search engine is likely to intercept this search and ask you to edit it. If you go ahead, you are likely to end up with an unmanageable amount of material.
Employment dismissal	This is likely to result in a significant number of hits which you can then scroll through to find the ones relevant to you. Again, this is possibly rather time consuming.
Employment dismissal transfer	This should result in a smaller and more manageable number of hits which you can then review and select as appropriate.
Employment dismissal transfer business undertaking	If you search on these terms, you will probably end up with a manageable number of hits if you search so that all elements have to be present. If you search so that any of these elements are to be present in any result, you will end up with too much data.
Employment dismissal transfer 'business undertaking'	Including the phrase 'business undertaking' in quotes or brackets is likely to cause problems. The legislation in this area does not use the phrase 'business undertaking', only 'undertaking', so this would eliminate information that would be highly useful to you. Be careful of specific phrases unless you are sure that they are correct. A possible alternative approach would be to search with the phrase in quotes and then to carry out a second search without the quotes to check if anything has been missed.

Essentially, you are trying to strike a balance between being so specific that you miss things and so general that you waste time. As you become more experienced, you will find this task easier, partly because you will know the resource better and partly because you will have a deeper knowledge of your areas of practice – an employment lawyer would, for example, know that the phrase 'transfer of undertaking' would provide access to a number of useful references on the topic considered above.

When you are recording your research, make a note of your search terms and the steps you followed from the results. If you need to go back and retrace your steps, you will be able to do so easily. You will also have contemporaneous notes of your path so that it can be easily written up to show a complete record of your research. Some resources offer a 'research trail' facility where they show you where you went during that particular enquiry. This is helpful, but you should always be prepared to make some notes of your own, for example what was useful about the paragraphs or sections that you found and their implications for your client's matter.

Summary Points

- Select your electronic resource carefully; some can be misleading or even incorrect
- Be careful about which version of a statute you are considering. Some sites only print the version as originally passed
- Consider your search terms carefully. If you are too specific, you may have no hits; too vague and you may have thousands
- Use connectors in your searches to narrow down the number of hits
- Use quotation marks to search for particular phrases
- Your resource should provide some guidance on how to use connectors and on searching. Check them and use any tutorials available

---

7.4.2 Paper resources

The paper resources you have available to you will also vary depending on your firm or LPC provider, but you should always have access to *Halsbury's Laws*. You will find during your LPC that you will be using practitioner texts, possibly for the first time. These will differ from the academic texts that you may have been used to and using them may require some adjustment. Again, what you have available to you will vary, but common examples include *Archbold's Criminal Practice*, the Civil Procedure Rules (the 'White Book'), Woodfall *The Law of Landlord and Tenant*, Wilkinson's *Road Traffic* and the Orange and Yellow Tax Handbooks.

The temptation is to begin with your LPC textbook. This will not help you to familiarize yourself with the practitioner texts that you will be expected to use in practice. Your LPC is the time to find your way around the main practitioner texts, where you can ask your librarian or tutors for help if you are struggling. The solicitor supervising you will expect you to know your way around these resources and is unlikely to be impressed if you cannot use them and have to rely on your LPC manual (which will by then be out of date!).

Some of these will be traditional bound books, others will be looseleaf works. You need to know your way around a law library and the best way to get to know how to use these resources is to practise using them.

Halsbury's Laws is probably the most commonly available paper resource. It is an excellent starting point, but should not be your finishing point as well! As we shall consider later, *Halsbury's Laws* is not a primary resource but commentary, and you should therefore follow up any references to statute or case law once you have checked for updates. This will enable you to look in detail at the wording of the statute or the facts of the case to determine their relevance to your client's matter. For example, in exercise 3, the issue of interpretation is considered in some detail and the wording of the statute is critical to giving correct advice.

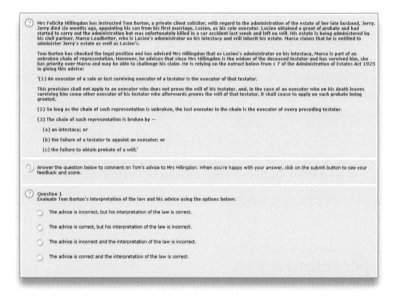

Searching paper resources

The technique for searching paper resources is different from that used in searching electronic resources, although clearly there are overlaps. For example, you will need to start with an index, whatever type of paper resource you are using.

In exercise 2, for example, you will be asked to compile a flowchart of the path you would take when using *Halsbury's Laws* as your resource for a piece of research.

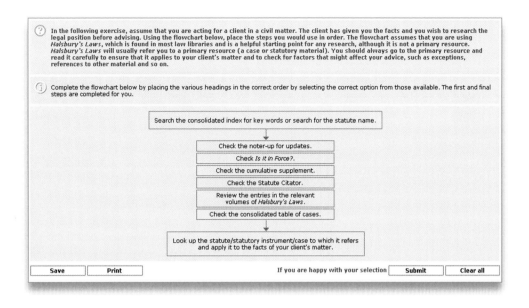

In paper-based research (and it is of course possible to use both types of resource together to research a problem), your approach to searching will be slightly different. If you are using a single, bound work, you would usually expect to find a number of different indices.

For example, you will generally find:

- An index of legislation
- An index of cases
- A more conventional index of the work itself

If you know the statutory provision or case that you want, you can look up any references to it in these indices. As you become more experienced, you may well find that you use this type of index more because you are looking up particular points about a legal issue you may already have come across in practice. Where you are searching for something that is less familiar, your first step will usually be to check the general index. In a looseleaf or multi-volume work, you should have an index to each volume, plus a consolidated index to the entire work. You should use the consolidated index to direct you to the correct volume and paragraphs, rather than checking several indices of individual volumes to find what you want and wasting time.

You will also generally find entries and sub-entries in the conventional index of any work. For example, if we use the previous unfair dismissal example, the index is likely to group them as follows:

> **Example**
>
> EMPLOYMENT
>   Unfair dismissal
>   Transfer of undertaking

You will almost certainly find that the first few exercises that you attempt will require you to experiment with the use of the indices, but practice should help with this and you will get quicker as the resource and the experience of researching becomes more familiar.

Once you follow up the entries in the individual volumes or parts of the bound work to which the index has directed you, you should review the information and make sure that you pay close attention to any notes. The notes will give authority for any statements and refer you to other paragraphs and primary sources such as cases or statutes. Unless they are obviously not relevant, it is generally good practice to follow up any such references once you have checked that they are up to date (more on this later). You should always review any primary sources so that you ensure that the wording of the legislation or the facts of your case apply to your client's matter.

As we considered earlier, *Halsbury's Laws* is possibly the most commonly available paper resource. It is also available as an electronic resource. It is an excellent place to start, although it is important to remember that it is a secondary, not a primary source of law. You should therefore follow up any references to statute and case law that you find in any of the various volumes.

The interactive exercises include an exercise on how to use *Halsbury's Laws* using a flowchart. You will need to attempt this exercise before you carry out the research exercises to give you a clear picture of how to use this resource.

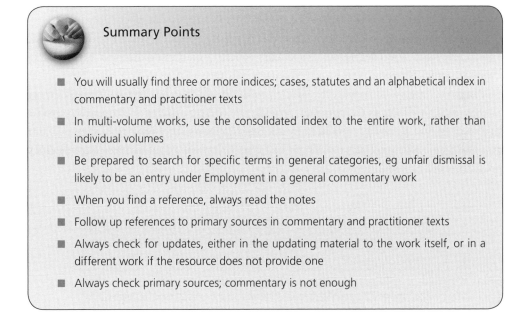

Summary Points

- You will usually find three or more indices; cases, statutes and an alphabetical index in commentary and practitioner texts

- In multi-volume works, use the consolidated index to the entire work, rather than individual volumes

- Be prepared to search for specific terms in general categories, eg unfair dismissal is likely to be an entry under Employment in a general commentary work

- When you find a reference, always read the notes

- Follow up references to primary sources in commentary and practitioner texts

- Always check for updates, either in the updating material to the work itself, or in a different work if the resource does not provide one

- Always check primary sources; commentary is not enough

7.5 Sources

7.5.1 Secondary sources

The section includes a number of references to primary and secondary sources. Primary sources are considered in the next paragraph, but secondary sources are also worth considering so that their place in your research is clear. Secondary sources such as practitioner texts, *Halsbury's Laws* and other commentary works are a good starting point. They give you an overview of the area of law in which you are conducting your research. They will often also lead you to explore other possibilities which you had not considered and help eliminate others which turn out not to be relevant. The notes to any entry should always be reviewed as they will often provide useful information.

Although secondary resources are an excellent starting point, they are not enough in themselves. A secondary source such as *Halsbury's Laws* will give authority for a statement, such as a case or statute. Once you have checked for any updates, you should then look at the primary source itself. Relying solely on a secondary source is bad practice and is likely to cause you problems with your assessments and with your research in practice.

7.5.2 Primary sources

As we have already considered briefly, research that begins and ends in an LPC textbook will not impress your assessor or your firm. As discussed, you need to look at the primary sources of law: statutory material and cases. Many practitioner texts can also be cited as authority, but you should always look to statutory material or cases where possible.

Interpreting cases and statutory material is a skill in which you should have some experience from your degree or conversion course. You should harness this skill in Practical Legal Research and ensure that you can interpret what you find. Remember that in many cases, a subsection can have a profound effect, so be careful when reviewing provisions which look as though they provide the correct answer. It is entirely possible that they do, but if they are qualified by a subsection or another provision, they may not give the whole picture. For example, in exercise 3, you are asked to interpret statutory provisions in a case study.

Mrs Felicity Hillingdon has instructed Tom Burton, a private client solicitor, with regard to the administration of the estate of her late husband, Jerry. Jerry died six months ago, appointing his son from his first marriage, Lucien, as his sole executor. Lucien obtained a grant of probate and had started to carry out the administration but was unfortunately killed in a car accident last week and left no will. His estate is being administered by his civil partner, Marco Leadbetter, who is Lucien's administrator on his intestacy and will inherit his estate. Marco claims that he is entitled to administer Jerry's estate as well as Lucien's.

Tom Burton has checked the legal position and has advised Mrs Hillingdon that as Lucien's administrator on his intestacy, Marco is part of an unbroken chain of representation. However, he advises that since Mrs Hillingdon is the widow of the deceased testator and has survived him, she has priority over Marco and may be able to challenge his claim. He is relying on the extract below from s 7 of the Administration of Estates Act 1925 in giving this advice:

'(1) An executor of a sole or last surviving executor of a testator is the executor of that testator.

This provision shall not apply to an executor who does not prove the will of his testator, and, in the case of an executor who on his death leaves surviving him some other executor of his testator who afterwards proves the will of that testator, it shall cease to apply on such probate being granted.

(2) So long as the chain of such representation is unbroken, the last executor in the chain is the executor of every preceding testator.

(3) The chain of such representation is broken by —

(a) an intestacy; or

(b) the failure of a testator to appoint an executor; or

(c) the failure to obtain probate of a will;'

Answer the question below to comment on Tom's advice to Mrs Hillingdon. When you're happy with your answer, click on the submit button to see your feedback and score.

Question 1
Evaluate Tom Burton's interpretation of the law and his advice using the options below:

○ The advice is incorrect, but his interpretation of the law is correct.

○ The advice is correct, but his interpretation of the law is incorrect.

○ The advice is incorrect and the interpretation of the law is incorrect.

○ The advice is correct and the interpretation of the law is correct.

Different parts of the same section may give exceptions to a general rule in some circumstances. Provisions elsewhere in the same or a different statute may mean that the rule that you have found does not apply in your client's case. Check the notes to the section that you have found and follow up relevant cross-references or provisions which appear to qualify the section.

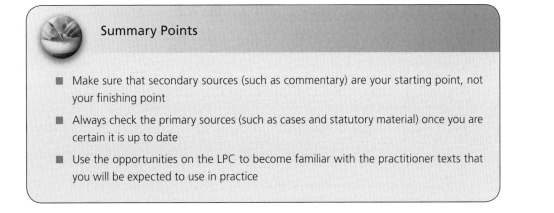

Summary Points

- Make sure that secondary sources (such as commentary) are your starting point, not your finishing point
- Always check the primary sources (such as cases and statutory material) once you are certain it is up to date
- Use the opportunities on the LPC to become familiar with the practitioner texts that you will be expected to use in practice

7.6 Research paths

Showing your path to the answer you are presenting is rather like showing your workings in a mathematical problem. In your assessment, you will need to demonstrate that you have grounds for the answer you give and have shown an understanding of the process and resources that you have used as well as your client's problem (real or fictitious), for your assessment. If you cannot show how you have arrived at your answer, you cannot show that you have authority for what you say. In an assessment, an answer with no credible research path leading up to it is open to allegations of plagiarism (as we considered in more detail earlier). It is also unlikely to be assessed as competent since the research path is an important part of what is being assessed.

A clear research path should take your reader through the process. It should show:

- Where you went
- How you got there
- Why the information addresses your client's problem

There should be no 'jumps', where the logical progression from one step to another is not apparent. As we will consider when we look at presenting your results, you will not necessarily wish to include every small detail, running to several pages, but you should include enough to allow your reader to see where you have been and how you got to the relevant information.

For example, in exercise 5, you are taken through how to present your research path as part of the presentation of your results.

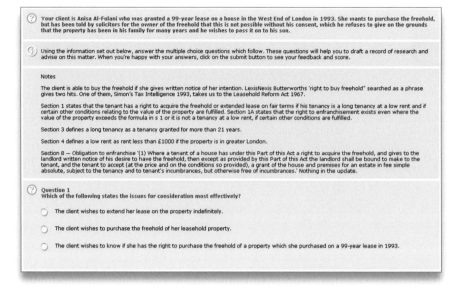

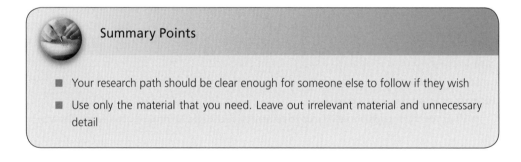

You will also find exercises on writing research memos in the Writing and Drafting module.

Summary Points

■ Your research path should be clear enough for someone else to follow if they wish

■ Use only the material that you need. Leave out irrelevant material and unnecessary detail

7.7 Updating

Always check whether what you have found is current law. If it is out of date, you will give wrong advice and will almost certainly be negligent if you could have checked but didn't.

There are various methods of updating, depending on which resource you are using. 'Is it in force?' and various citators will tell you whether statutes and other material are current law and whether they have been amended. There is an example of updating as part of the research process in exercise 2 where you are asked to compile a flowchart of the research process using *Halsbury's Laws* and *Halsbury's Statutes*.

Even if you are certain that nothing has changed, always check and say that you have checked. Law changes constantly, with new cases and statutory measures contributing to the legal landscape all the time. It is better to state that you checked, for example 'Is it in force?' and found nothing than to say nothing and leave your reader with doubts. This is particularly important for your assessment. In *Halsbury's Laws* and *Halsbury's Statutes*, for example, there are various different places to look for updates. These include:

- The Consolidated Table of Cases (which gives you information on whether a case is still good law and cross-refers to other cases in which it has been cited or distinguished)

- The Statute Citator (which tells you whether a statute or section has been amended or repealed)

- The Cumulative Supplement (this gives you updates by paragraph of *Halsbury's Laws*, not chronologically or by area)

- 'Is it in force?' (this tells you when statutes came into force)

- The noter-up (this is an additional updating service which should be used together with the Cumulative Supplement)

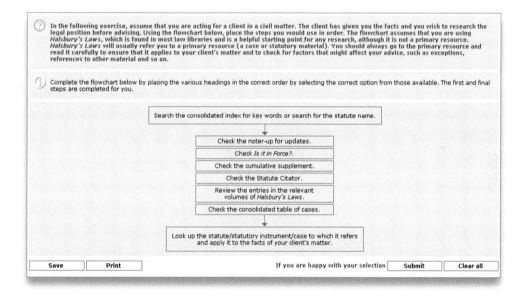

For electronic resources, check the 'update' or 'stop press' if there is one. Often, the resource will alert you to the fact that there are relevant updates. Always follow these up and, again, say that you did so, even if they turn out to make no difference to your overall conclusions. Remember that it is possible to use both electronic and paper sources for your research. You may therefore also wish to check for updates using an electronic resource if you have access to one. Many bound copy and looseleaf practitioner texts now have CD-Rom versions and companion websites. If they do, check them to ensure that there are no additional updates that affect your research.

> ### Summary Points
>
> - Always check for updates before reviewing the primary source
> - Always state that you checked for updates and where you did so, even if you found nothing relevant
> - Remember that for many resources there are several sources of updating material
> - For some resources, such as bound books, you may have to check for an update in another work. It is perfectly acceptable to check for updates to a paper resource in an electronic one, if necessary

7.8 Your conclusions

Always come to some conclusion, even if it consists of offering options and stating the consequences of each option in turn. Be careful of being too lengthy in your conclusions and bringing in other, more academic points. Remember that in practice, your reader is busy. They want to see your conclusions easily, without having to wade through large amounts of information. Consider using bullet points to summarize your conclusions if there are several points. You also need to ensure that you state how the law applies to the facts, not just give a statement of the law. Give the implications of what you have discovered and be as clear as possible. For example, Exercise 5 looks at what to do with the results of a piece of research where you have the information, but need to consider how to present them.

Your client is Anisa Al-Fulani who was granted a 99-year lease on a house in the West End of London in 1993. She wants to purchase the freehold, but has been told by solicitors for the owner of the freehold that this is not possible without his consent, which he refuses to give on the grounds that the property has been in his family for many years and he wishes to pass it on to his son.

Using the information set out below, answer the multiple choice questions which follow. These questions will help you to draft a record of research and advise on this matter. When you're happy with your answers, click on the submit button to see your feedback and score.

Notes

The client is able to buy the freehold if she gives written notice of her intention. LexisNexis Butterworths 'right to buy freehold' searched as a phrase gives two hits. One of them, Simon's Tax Intelligence 1993, takes us to the Leasehold Reform Act 1967.

Section 1 states that the tenant has a right to acquire the freehold or extended lease on fair terms if his tenancy is a long tenancy at a low rent and if certain other conditions relating to the value of the property are fulfilled. Section 1A states that the right to enfranchisement exists even where the value of the property exceeds the formula in s 1 or it is not a tenancy at a low rent, if certain other conditions are fulfilled.

Section 3 defines a long tenancy as a tenancy granted for more than 21 years.

Section 4 defines a low rent as rent less than £1000 if the property is in greater London.

Section 8 — Obligation to enfranchise '(1) Where a tenant of a house has under this Part of this Act a right to acquire the freehold, and gives to the landlord written notice of his desire to have the freehold, then except as provided by this Part of this Act the landlord shall be bound to make to the tenant, and the tenant to accept (at the price and on the conditions so provided), a grant of the house and premises for an estate in fee simple absolute, subject to the tenancy and to tenant's incumbrances, but otherwise free of incumbrances.' Nothing in the update.

Question 1
Which of the following states the issues for consideration most effectively?

○ The client wishes to extend her lease on the property indefinitely.

○ The client wishes to purchase the freehold of her leasehold property.

○ The client wishes to know if she has the right to purchase the freehold of a property which she purchased on a 99-year lease in 1993.

7.9 Advice

Advice does not consist of ordering your client or the solicitor who is supervising you to do something. In many matters, there will be more than one option and you will be trying to give the client enough information to make an informed choice about how to deal with their matter. If there are various options, set them out with a brief statement of what is involved and the consequences of each option. If you know the client's attitude to risk, rank them in order, possibly with the most appropriate option first.

Make sure that your advice is appropriate. Often the least interesting option from your point of view will be the most acceptable to your client. Remember that the SRA Code of Conduct requires that you act in the client's best interest, however useful another option might be for your own experience! You also need to ensure that the advice you give is practical and takes into account your client's objectives or requirements.

Summary Points

- Always reach a conclusion and state it clearly
- If there are various options, set them out with the consequences of each one
- Be as brief as you can. Don't repeat everything you have already written
- When giving advice, it must be appropriate and in the client's best interests
- Be practical; take into account what your client wants or needs
- Apply the law to the facts. However well you state the law, if you don't apply it, you are not advising

---

7.9.1 Presenting your advice

Your firm is likely to have a house style for presenting research. Some firms use a grid for the various pieces of information, others will want you to write a memo. Whichever it is, ensure that what you say is clear, logical and easy to read. Using headings and bullet points is generally helpful, although if you overuse them, you will make the text difficult to read. The exercises set out at the end of this section use the format below, but be guided by your LPC provider for your assessment and your firm during your training contract. Remember that the headings and the order in which those headings appear are likely to vary.

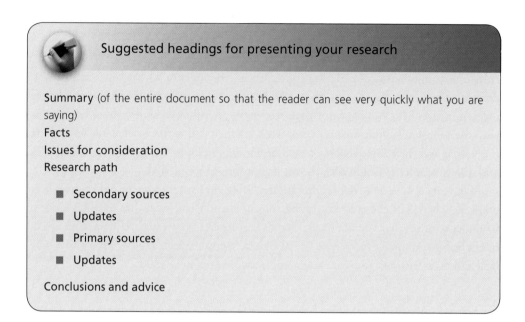

Suggested headings for presenting your research

Summary (of the entire document so that the reader can see very quickly what you are saying)
Facts
Issues for consideration
Research path

- Secondary sources
- Updates
- Primary sources
- Updates

Conclusions and advice

Generally, any research findings that you present should follow the principles of good writing, and this is covered in more detail in the Writing and Drafting module, which includes exercises on writing research memos. The aim is to be as clear as possible and to give your reader a document which is logical, easy to follow and comes to a sound conclusion based on the law and facts as stated.

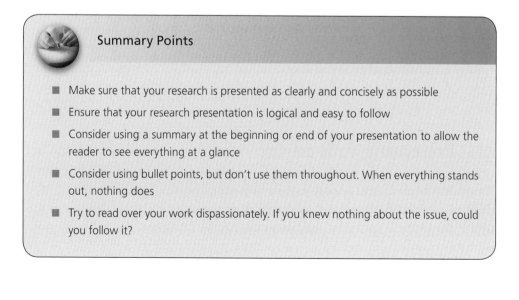

Summary Points

- Make sure that your research is presented as clearly and concisely as possible
- Ensure that your research presentation is logical and easy to follow
- Consider using a summary at the beginning or end of your presentation to allow the reader to see everything at a glance
- Consider using bullet points, but don't use them throughout. When everything stands out, nothing does
- Try to read over your work dispassionately. If you knew nothing about the issue, could you follow it?

7.10 **Costs and assessments**

In practice, costs are a factor in everything that you do. You cannot spend vast amounts of time on a matter if you will not be able to pass on the costs by billing the client for that time. Balance the need to be thorough in your research with the need to avoid wasting costs.

During your LPC, you will have a finite amount of time in which to complete your assessment. If you spend many hours on a piece of research, you will not be keeping up with other work. Again, you need to balance thoroughness with practicality.

7.11 **Conclusion**

Practical Legal Research is an important skill for you to master, both for the purposes of your assessment during your LPC and for your training contract. Remember that the approach is not an academic one. Trying to present your research in the form of an essay will waste your time and that of your reader. Be guided by your LPC provider and your firm as to how you should present information for these purposes, but be aware that the focus must always be on applying the law to the facts of your client's case. If you focus firmly on this viewpoint throughout, you will avoid wasting time on unproductive digressions.

7.12 **The exercises**

The following exercises on research method and research paths should be attempted after having completed exercises 1–5 inclusive in the Practical Legal Research online module. Exercises 1–5 deal with research method and lead into the practice exercises set out here. They are included in the section to give you flexibility when conducting your research. Obviously for paper resources, having a hard copy is useful as you can take it with you. For electronic resources, it avoids the need for you to have several windows open at once, which can slow down your computer, especially if you are using dial-up.

The exercises are divided into paper and electronic resources, with the paper resources first. Attempt each question and write up your answer before going online to check it. The exercises will ask you a series of questions about what you found and how. You can then download a suggested answer. It is very likely that the suggested answer will not look exactly the same as yours. For example, you may have used a different resource. When comparing the suggested answer with yours consider whether they differ in a fundamental way (such as a different conclusion or advice). Consider whether your research pathway is logical, with no gaps, whether your answer is up to date (and you have stated that you checked that it was current) and whether you have correctly understood the facts, law and the client's objectives. If you are unsure, speak to your tutor.

Remember that the exercises focus on research method and research paths. Be guided by your LPC provider or your firm on how they require you to present your research. As discussed, the Writing and Drafting module provides examples of how you might present your findings in the form of a memo.

There are ten exercises altogether, five on electronic and five on paper resources. You do not need to have completed all the exercises before you check them online. You may wish to complete one, check it and then go on to the next. Remember that the law may change between the time *LPC Skills Online* goes to press and the time you carry out the exercise. Check the updates for each exercise to see if there is anything new by clicking on the 'What's new' button.

7.13 The questions

Answer the following questions using PAPER resources. You may either complete all exercises and use the online exercises to review each one in turn, or complete and review them one at a time. They can only be reviewed in the order in which they appear below.

Problem 1
Your client is Kayoko Nita. She is a Japanese national, but is resident in the UK at the moment. She is studying on the LPC and will be starting her training contract in Leeds on completion of that course. She is currently working as a translator and is earning fairly significant amounts – far more than her friends – due to a relatively high hourly rate. She is aware that her friends are paying tax once their earnings are more than the personal allowance, which she understands they can earn before having to pay any tax. She has come to see you because she is worried about whether she should also be paying income tax on the money she earns. Advise her.

Problem 2
You are a trainee solicitor in Greenbay Hudson. You read in the local news recently that a client, James Mulden, whose litigation work you did last year, has recently been arrested. He had been producing counterfeit goods and is described by the article as having links to organized crime. At the time you carried out the work, you were suspicious of the client but decided not to make an authorized disclosure under s338 of the Proceeds of Crime act 2002 as the information that you had from your client was privileged. You then continued to act in the transaction, which has no connection with the matters on which he has been arrested. What is your position?

Problem 3
You have been consulted by Janneke and Petrus Metternich regarding the estate of their mother, Mrs Doortje Metternich, who died last week. Mrs Metternich was intestate. She and her husband separated twenty years ago, but had never divorced. She was considering obtaining a judicial separation at the time of her death, but had not taken any steps to obtain one. Janneke and Petrus have not seen their father for

many years and do not want him to have a share of their mother's estate. He has written to say that he does not want to administer the estate, but he wants anything to which he might be entitled. The whole family is UK resident and domiciled. Advise them.

Problem 4
You have been asked to advise a client, Chris Forrester, a UK national, regarding his entitlement to Disability Living Allowance. He currently claims this in the UK, but wants to move to Germany to be near his sister who married a German man and is living in Düsseldorf. He will not be able to move if it means losing his benefit. Advise him.

Problem 5
You have been consulted by Chinua Boadu who has invented a form of combustion engine which he considers will revolutionize car manufacture as it is carbon neutral. He has patented his idea and has backers from the car manufacturing industry who are keen to take his idea into production. He wants his Member of Parliament to put forward a proposal that cars with his new engine should have tax incentives from the state to encourage people to buy them, rather than buying from competitors elsewhere in the EU, as this would be better for the environment. He does not know if such tax incentives are permitted by law. Advise him.

Answer the following questions using ELECTRONIC resources. You may either complete all exercises and use the online exercises to review each one in turn, or complete and review them one at a time. They can only be reviewed in the order in which they appear below.

Problem 6
You are acting for Martha Framwell, who has asked you to act in her conveyancing matter. She is buying the house from a family friend, John Phipps. He is a widower with no children and he is selling because he feels that the house is too big for one person. They have exchanged contracts, but agreed a completion date of one month after exchange as this suited both parties. Although they are close friends, Mrs Framwell is paying full market value for the house. Unfortunately, Mr Phipps has recently had serious problems with his business and between exchange and completion he was made bankrupt. Mrs Framwell has received a letter stating that the title to the property has passed to the trustee in bankruptcy. Advise her.

Problem 7
You are acting for Bartomeu Ferrer, who runs a wine importation and mail order business. He has fewer than 25 employees, who are managed by Mark Newsome. Mark recently had an affair with another employee, which caused very bad feeling among the workforce. As a result, business has been disrupted. Mr Ferrer cannot afford to allow this disruption to continue and would like Mr Newsome to leave his employ. He is prepared to make him a generous offer if he leaves, although there is nothing in the contract of employment which allows him to do this. Mr Newsome has indicated that he would be prepared to agree to this as he would like to start his own business and is finding the atmosphere at work almost unbearable. He would not be prepared to resign without any payment as he would not be able to start his own business without any capital. Mr Ferrer has heard that it is possible to make

a payment of up to £30,000 tax-free to an employee who leaves by agreement. He also wants Mr Newsome to give up his right to sue later for his dismissal and wants him to sign some sort of agreement confirming that he will not take Mr Ferrer to a tribunal. Advise Mr Ferrer.

Problem 8

You are acting for Polina Fyodorova who is setting up two companies in the UK. She manufactures and imports traditional Russian toys for sale in the UK. One of the companies (Matrioshka Limited) would be a trading company, dealing with the running of shops and outlets in larger stores. The other company (Matrioshka Wholesales Limited) will deal with the importation process and wholesale operations. Matrioshka Wholesales Limited will be a wholly owned subsidiary of Matrioshka Limited. She also wants to set up a subsidiary of Matrioshka Limited in Russia which would deal with the export side of her operations – Matrioshka (Moscow) Limited. She is unclear about whether the accounts of the Russian subsidiary would also have to be submitted to Companies House along with the accounts of the UK companies in the group. Advise her.

Problem 9

You have had an initial meeting with Ofelia Corazao regarding a breach of contract on which she would like to sue. The other party is a Belgian national, resident in Belgium. Ofelia is a British citizen who is habitually resident in the UK. The contract is silent as to which law should apply, but Ofelia was contracted to carry out work under the terms of the contract in England. Advise her.

Problem 10

You are acting for Thomas Richards, who is in prison after having been convicted of armed robbery. Recently, his argument with another prisoner ended in violence and Mr Richards is now confined to his cell for a period of 28 days. This is not the first time Mr Richards has been violent towards fellow inmates and the prison governor is concerned to prevent further violence. Mr Richards has been reading up on human rights legislation and wants you to investigate the possibility of using the Human Rights Act to challenge his treatment and possibly obtain compensation for him. Advise him.

Index

A

advising *see also*
> **interviewing**
Code of Conduct 90, 105
commercial factors 89
difficult questions 89, 90
jargon 87, 88, 91 *see also*
> **jargon**
lack of knowledge 90, 91
legal position 87, 88
misconceptions 87
private client matters 89
professional conduct 89
relevant facts 87
advocacy
advocacy skills
> importance 124
> persuasion 98, 109
> presentations 98
> Solicitors Regulation
> > Authority (SRA) 98
> speaking in court 106
closing speeches
> essential principles 121
> exercises 121
> objective 121
ethics
> client's best
> > interests 105
> Code of Conduct 90,
> > 105
> duty to the court 105,
> > 106
exercises 98, 101
hearings *see* **hearings**
opening speeches
> civil cases 114
> contents 114, 115
> credibility 114
> delivery 115
> essential principles 115
> "mind maps" 115, 116

note cards 115
overview
> adversarial system 98
> contentious work 98
> court etiquette 98, 112,
> > 113
persuasion
> clarity 111, 112
> ethical
> > considerations 109
> example 110
> gestures, use of 107, 109,
> > 111
> interpretation of
> > facts 109
> key points, use of 111
> misleading the
> > court 109, 110
> presentation of
> > argument 111
> simplicity 111, 112
pleas in mitigation
> clarity 122
> criminal offences 122
> purpose 122
preparation
> affidavits 105
> case management sys-
> > tems 105, 106
> case planning 98, 99,
> > 102, 104
> checklists 101, 106
> civil matters 100
> client instructions 100
> criminal matters 100
> diary system 104
> disputed wills 101, 102
> essential principles 105
> exercises 101
> family law matters 101,
> > 102
> importance 98, 106, 124

> information
> > requirements 101
> initial interview 100
> key facts 100
> list of witnesses 100
> method 101
> subject matter 100
> timelines 102, 103
> witness statements 105
speaking in court
> advocacy skills 106
> clarity 109
> confidence 124
> essential principles 107,
> > 109
> eye contact 107
> gestures 107, 109, 111
> mannerisms 107, 109
> nerves, dealing
> > with 106, 107
> performance 109
> practising 106
> technique 106
> tone of voice 107
> voice pitch 107, 109
> volume 107
affidavits
attendance notes 43
> *see also* **attendance**
> **notes**
case preparation 105
attendance notes *see also*
> **note-taking**
affidavits 43
content 43, 45, 47
court hearings 43
criminal matters 43
notes of meetings 43, 45,
> 92, 95
purpose 43, 45
relevant detail 43
sitting behind counsel 46

attendance notes *see also*
note-taking (*Cont.*)
telephone attendance
notes 45, 46
witness statements 43

B

bail applications
human rights issues 114
procedure 114
right to bail 114
boilerplate
use, of 60 *see also* **drafting**

C

case management systems
use, of 68, 92, 105, 106
case planning *see also* **case
management systems**
preparation 98, 99, 102,
104
timelines 102, 106
citing authority *see also* **legal
writing**
client letters 33, 34
example 33
professional advice 33
proper citation 34
record of research 33
requirement, for 33
specific authority 33
clients
advising *see* **advising**
client care 39, 40, 75, 76
client instructions 100
client letters 31–4, 36, 39,
40, 75, 76
client's best interests 105,
147
conflict checks 75
dispute resolution
advice 100 *see also*
dispute resolution
identity 75
interviewing 72, 75–9,
85, 86 *see also*
interviewing
legal research needs
client
considerations 128–30

client objectives 131,
132, 147
private client matters 89
court hearings *see* **hearings**
cross-examination
examination in chief 117,
118
exercises 120, 121
purpose 119
questions
closed questions 119,
120
leading questions 119
open questions 119, 120

D

dispute resolution
Civil Procedure Rule
(CPR) 100
client advice 100
options available 100
requirement 100
documents (drafting)
amending documents
checking
amendments 62
computer use 62
confidentiality 62
negotiating amend-
ments 64, 65
proofreading 62, 65
secretarial support 62
tracking changes 62,
63, 65
transactional
drafting 63–5
consistency 66, 67
contradiction 66
cross-references
function 65
need, for 65, 67
proofreading 66
renumbered
paragraphs 66
definition section
commercial
documents 55
contradictory
definitions 56
examples 55

letters 55
purpose 55
engrossments 64
final version 64
interim stages 64
legal documents 53
linked documents 67
litigation documents 64
proofreading 62, 64, 65
transactional
drafting 63–5
wills 64
documents (generally)
content 53, 54
drafting *see* **documents
(drafting)**
effect 56
function 54
legal documents 53
linked documents 67
litigation documents 64
meaning 56
operative clause 54, 56
precedents *see* **precedents**
property-related
documents 63
structure
body of document 54
definition section 54, 55
introduction 54
schedules 54
transactional drafting 63,
64
drafting
ambiguity 52, 53, 57
bespoke documents 52
boilerplates 60
clarity 52, 53, 55, 57
computer use 52
consequences
careful consideration 56,
57
meaning/effect of
documents 56
meeting objectives 57
differing approaches 52
differing situations 52
documents *see* **documents
(drafting)**
drafting skill 52, 70

exercises 70
forms *see* **forms**
leases 52, 57
litigation matters 52
negligence claims (poor
    drafting) 53
precedents, use of 52,
    56–62 *see also*
    precedents
procedural approach 52
professional changes 52
punctuation 52, 53
separate assessment 52
time/cost issues 52, 53
training period, during 52

E

email
attachments 47
drafting 47
essential principles 47
format 47
letters sent, by 36
notification services 133
printing off 47
"reply all" function 47
style 47
text abbreviations 47
tone 47
ethics
client's best interests 105
Code of Conduct 90, 105
duty to the court 105, 106

F

feedback
different kinds 14
importance 14
interactive exercises 6, 10
    see also **interactive**
    exercises
reflective learning 14,
    18 *see also* **reflective**
    learning
forms
case management
    systems 68
company commercial
    work 67
completion of forms 67–9

correct form 69
electronic completion 68
essential principles 69
explanatory notes 69
HM Revenue and
    Customs 68
Laserforms package 68
proofreading 68
property work 67, 68
RIRO principle (rubbish
    in/rubbish out) 68
tax forms 67

G

grammar/spelling/punc-
    tuation *see also* **legal**
    writing
computer spellchecker 27,
    49
context 27
importance 27, 28

H

hearings
applications for costs 112
bail applications
    human rights issues 114
    procedure 114
    right to bail 114
closing speeches
    essential principles 121
    exercises 121
    objective 121
costs (civil matters)
    application for costs 123
    interim hearings 122
    overall costs 123
    responsibility 122, 123
County Court 112
court etiquette 98, 112,
    113
cross-examination
    closed questions 119,
        120
    examination in
        chief 117, 118
    exercises 120, 121
    leading questions 119
    open questions 119, 120
    purpose 119

examination in chief
    civil matters 116
    closed questions 118
    criminal matters 116
    cross-examination 117,
        118
    leading questions 117,
        119
    open questions 117
follow up 123
hearings in chambers 112
High Court 112
interim applications 112
Magistrates' Court 112
opening speeches
    civil cases 114
    contents 114, 115
    credibility 114
    delivery 115
    essential principles 115
    "mind maps" 115, 116
    note cards 115
opposing side
    examinations 119, 124
speeches 119, 124
pleas in mitigation
    clarity 122
    criminal offences 122
    purpose 122
questions
    closed questions 118,
        119, 120
    cross-examination 117,
        118
    leading questions 117,
        119
    open questions 117, 119,
        120
    technique 116
rights of audience 112, 113
telephone hearings 112,
    113
witnesses
    examination, of 116–8
    witness statements 119

I

interactive exercises
case study exercises 8
emphasis, on 2

interactive exercises (*Cont.*)
  exercise maps 6
  explanation 4–7
  feedback 6, 10, 14
  multiple choice exercises 2
  practical legal research *see
      also* **practical legal
      research**
    electronic research 7
    key words 7
    paper research 7
    research method 7
    use of resources 7
  purpose 5
  reflective diary 6 *see also*
      reflective diary
  scores 6, 9
  supplementary exercises 6,
      7, 9
  work method 9
interviewing *see also*
      advising
  clients
    client care 75, 76
    client contact 72
    client history 76
    client letters 75, 76
  conduct of interview
    beginning the
        interview 81
    body language 83, 84
    client's matter 77–9
    concluding the
        interview 92
    confidentiality 83
    criminal work 81
    emotional issues 82
    essential principles 82,
        83
    family law matters 82
    meeting room 81
    professional conduct
        issues 83
    tact 81
    telephone calls 83
    time/cost factors 84
    time keeping 80
    tone 81
  essential principles 77
  exercises 72–4

follow up
  administrative aspect 93
  attendance note 92, 95
  case management
      systems 92
  checklists 92, 95
  contacts 93
  documents 93
  key words, use of 93–5
  progress information 95
initial interview 100
interviewing skills 72,
    74, 95
legal issues 76
legal knowledge 72
note-taking
  checking facts 87
  client issues 85, 86
  format 85, 86
  method 85
  "mind maps" 86
objective 72
online course 72, 73
practical issues
  client care 75, 76
  client identity 75
  client letters 75, 76
  conflict checks 75
  money laundering
      issues 75
  professional conduct
      issues 75
preparation 74, 75
questions
  closed questions 79
  combination of
      questions 79, 80
  difficult questions 89, 90
  open questions 79, 80
  supplementary
      questions 80
Solicitors Regulation
    Authority (SRA)
  requirements 76
standards 72

J

jargon
  advising 87, 88, 91 *see also*
      advising

archaic terms 24, 25
example 24
French words 24
interviews 87, 88, 91 *see
    also* **interviewing**
Latin words 24, 25
meaning 24

L

learning
  active learning 12
  deep learning 12, 18
  individual approach 12
  learning style 12
  passive learning 5
  reading 5
  reflection 12, 13 *see also*
      reflective learning
  shallow learning 12, 18
legal knowledge
  importance 2
legal research *see* **practical
    legal research**
legal writing
  appropriate style 22
  assessment 20
  attendance notes *see*
      attendance notes
  audience
    appropriate style 30, 31
    audience
        comprehension 31
    different readers 30
    intended audience 30,
        31
  citing authority *see* **citing
      authority**
  clarity
    example 26
    importance 25, 28, 49
    length of sentences 25–8
  conclusions 49
  detailed brevity
    bullet points 20
    numbered lists 30
    presentation of
        argument 30
    record of research 30
    requirement 29
  email *see* **email**

exercises 49
further reading 49, 50
general rules 22
grammar/spelling/
   punctuation *see*
   grammar/spelling/
   punctuation
house style 48
jargon
   archaic terms 24, 25
   example 24
   French words 24
   Latin words 24, 25
   meaning 24
letters *see* **letters**
memos *see* **memos**
online exercises 49
overview
   different types/styles 22,
   23
   function 20
   key skill 20
   professional
      standards 20
plain English *see* **plain**
   English
practical aspects
   accuracy of typing 35
   attention to detail 49
   Dictaphone use 34
   dictation 34
   dictionary use 49
   digital dictation 35
   draft letters 35
   proofreading 34, 35,
      48, 49
   standard letters 35
   urgent work 34, 35
   voice recognition
      software 35
presenting research *see*
   presenting
   research
tone of writing
   client letters 31, 32
   contentious matters 32
   example 32
   formality 32
   importance 31
   informality 32

in-house
   communications 32
non-contentious
   matters 32
professional
   impression 31
word limits 22, 23
writing and drafting
   module 20, 21
letters *see also* **legal**
   writing
client care 39, 40
client letters 31–4, 36,
   39, 40
content
   body of letter 37
   final paragraph 38
   first paragraph 37
   headings 37
   key points 40
email 36 *see also* **email**
enclosures 38
forms of address 38, 39
plain English 40 *see also*
   plain English
references
   fee-earner
      identification 36
   file number 36
   standard format 36
   subject matter 36
   title 36
standard letters 35
style 36, 40
tone of letter 36, 40
LPC/skills assessment
advocacy 3, 8, 9 *see also*
   advocacy
assessment conditions 4
assessment criteria 3
drafting 3, 8, 9 *see also*
   drafting
interviewing 3, 8, 9 *see also*
   interviewing
legal writing 3, 8, 9, 20 *also*
   legal writing
method of assessment 3, 4
mock assessments 3, 4, 10
practical legal research 3,
   8, 9, 126 *see also*

practical legal
   research

M

memos *see also* **legal writing**
   executive summary 40
   headings 40
   key points 40
   presenting research 40,
      43 *see also* **presenting**
      research
   standard template 40
   subject matter 40

N

note-taking
   attendance notes *see*
      attendance notes
   checking facts 87
   client issues 85, 86
   format 85, 86
   legal research 128, 130 *see*
      also **practical legal**
      research
   method 85
   "mind maps" 86

P

plain English *see also* **legal**
   writing
   accuracy 28
   comprehension 23
   drafting 52, 53 *see also*
      drafting
   importance 23
   letter-writing 40 *see also*
      letters
   meaning 23, 24
   presenting research 41
      see also **presenting**
      research
   use, of 23, 25, 49
pleas in mitigation
   clarity 122
   criminal offences 122
   purpose 122
practical legal research
   advice-giving
      client's best interests 147
      client's objectives 147

practical legal research
   (*Cont.*)
   Code of Conduct 147
   house style 147
   informed choice 147
   options 147
   practical advice 147
   presentation 147, 148
   risk considerations 147
   summaries, use of 148
assessments 126
conclusions
   exercise 146
   format 146
   need, for 146
   presentation 146
essential principle 126
exercises 126, 127, 149, 150
indices
   case index 139–41
   index of
     legislation 139–41
   subject index 139–41
key words
   areas of law 132
   client's objectives 132
   practical steps 133
   use, of 131, 132
practical context
   client's objectives 131
   confidentiality 131
   cost factors 149
   professional conduct
     issues 131
   requests for
     research 130, 131
practical points
   "blind alleys" 129
   client
     considerations 128–30
   conclusions 130
   cost issues 128, 130
   cutting and pasting 129,
     130
   note-taking 128, 130
   online sources 129
   plagiarism 129, 130
   time factors 128
presenting research *see*
   presenting research

problem questions 150–2
record of research 30, 33,
   126
research paths
   exercises 143, 144
   function 143
   importance 143
   logical progression 143
   presentation 42
resources (electronic)
   email notification
     services 133
   government
     departments 134
   Lexis/Nexis
     Butterworths 133
   regulatory bodies 134
   searches 135–7
   updating 145
   useful websites 134, 135
   Westlaw 133
resources (generally)
   electronic resources 133–7
   internet use 133
   library resources 133
   subscription services 135
resources (paper resources)
   *Archbold: Criminal
     Practice* 137
   *Civil Procedure Rules
     (White Book)* 137
   Halsbury's Laws 137, 138,
     140, 141, 145
   Halsbury's Statutes 145
   indices 139–41
   legal commentaries 138,
     141
   *Orange/Yellow Tax
     Handbooks* 137
   primary sources 138, 140,
     141
   searches 138–40
   *Wilkinson: Road
     Traffic* 137
   *Woodfall: Landlord and
     Tenant* 137
skills requirement 126, 128,
   149
sources of law
   interpretation 142

primary sources 138,
   140–3
secondary sources 141, 143
statutory material 129
technique 128, 129
updating
   electronic resources 145
   Halsbury's Laws 145
   Halsbury's Statutes 145
   law in force 144, 145
   methods 144
   research process 144
precedents
adapting precedents 59,
   60, 62
firm's own precedents 58,
   60–2
HM Revenue and
   Customs 61
house style 57, 60–2
internet sources 59
review, of 57
Solicitors Regulation
   Authority (SRA) 61
sources 58–61
specialist areas 59
updating 57
use, of 56, 58, 59
presenting research *see
   also* **practical legal
   research**
accuracy 43
clarity 43
conclusions 42, 43
copying and pasting
example 41, 43
memos 40, 43 *see also*
   memos
plain English 41 *see also*
   plain English
pressure of time 41
research paths 42
structure 41, 42

Q

questions
closed questions
   court hearings 118, 19,
     120
   example 79

intimidation 79
nature, of 79
combination of
  questions 79, 80
court hearings
  advocacy technique 116
  closed questions 118,
    119, 120
  cross-examination 117,
    118
  examination in
    chief 116–8
  leading questions 117, 119
  open questions 117, 119,
    120
difficult questions 89, 90
open questions 79, 80, 117,
    119, 120
supplementary
    questions 80

R

reading
  passive learning method 5
reflective diary
  format 13
  on line diary 15
  portfolios 13, 15, 16, 18
  purpose 12–14
  structure 12
  template for reflection 12,
    13, 15
  use, of 6, 17
reflective learning
  deep learning 12, 18
  feedback 14, 18
  reflection
    importance 12, 13, 17
    template for
      reflection 12, 13, 15
  reflective diary *see* reflective
    diary

research *see* **practical legal
    research**

S

skills
  advocacy skills
    persuasion 98, 109
    presentations 98
    Solicitors Regulation
      Authority (SRA) 98
    speaking in court 106
  assessment *see* **LPC/skills
    assessment**
  confidence
  importance, of 2, 4, 10
  interviewing skills 72,
    74, 95 *see also*
    interviewing
  legal knowledge 2
  practising skills
    interviewing
      competitions 10
    mooting 10
    pro bono work 10
  research findings
    drafting skills 2, 3
    information technology
      skills 2
    research ability 2
    writing style 2
    written English 2
  research skills 126, 128
    see also **practical legal
      research**
**Solicitors Regulation
    Authority (SRA)**
  client care 39
  client's best interests 105,
    147
  Code of Conduct 90, 105,
    147
  interviewing

requirements 76
standards 72
skills requirement 3
legal writing/drafting
  standards 20
precedents 61 *see also*
  precedents
written standards 98
sources of law
  interpretation 142
  primary sources 138, 140–3
  secondary sources 141, 143

T

timelines
  breach of contract
    cases 103, 104
  case planning 102, 106
  civil matters 103
  criminal matters 102, 103
  example 103

U

**UK Centre for Legal
    Education
    Research**
  research findings 2, 3

W

witnesses
  case preparation
    evidence 105
    lists of witness 100
  examination, of 116–8
  witness statements 105,
    119
**writing and drafting
    module** *see also*
    **drafting; legal
    writing**
  professional standards 20
  structure 21